CW00806618

RENT BOYS

BY THE SAME AUTHOR

English (published by McGill-Queen's University Press, Montreal and Kingston)

Don't Tell: The Sexual Abuse of Boys, 2002
Dead Boys Can't Dance, 2004

French (published by VLB Éditeur, Montreal)

Les enfants de la prostitution (with Denis Ménard), 1987
L'Homme désemparé, 1988
Les lendemains de la révolution sexuelle, 1990
Tous les hommes le font, 1991
La peur de l'autre en soi (edited with Daniel Welzer-Lang and Pierre Dutey), 1994
La mémoire du désir, 1995
Ça arrive aussi aux garçons, 1997
Éloge de la diversité sexuelle, 1999
Mort ou fif (with Simon Louis Lajeunesse), 2001
Travailleurs du sexe, 2003

Portuguese (published by Ediçoes Loyola, Sao Paulo)

O homem desamparado, 1994
O erotismo masculino, 1994

Rent Boys

The World of Male Sex Workers

MICHEL DORAIS

TRANSLATED BY
PETER FELDSTEIN

McGill-Queen's University Press
Montreal & Kingston · London · Ithaca

© McGill-Queen's University Press 2005
ISBN 0-7735–2902-0 (cloth)
ISBN 0-7735–2903-9 (paper)

Legal deposit second quarter 2005
Bibliothèque nationale du Québec

Printed in Canada on acid-free paper

Originally published in French as *Travailleurs du sexe* by VLB Éditeur,
2003.

McGill-Queen's University Press acknowledges the support of the
Canada Council for the Arts for our publishing program. We also
acknowledge the financial support of the Government of Canada
through the Book Publishing Industry Development Program (BPIDP)
for our publishing activities.

Thanks to Simon Louis Lajeunesse for his insightful contribution as a
research assistant.

Library and Archives Canada Cataloguing in Publication

Dorais, Michel, 1954-
 Rent boys: the world of male sex workers /
 Michel Dorais; translated by Peter Feldstein.

 Translation of: Travailleurs du sexe.
 Includes bibliographical references and index.
 ISBN 0-7735–2902-0 (bound).
 ISBN 0-7735–2903-9 (pbk.)

 1. Male prostitution. 2. Male prostitutes. 3. Male prostitution –
Case studies. 4. Male prostitution – Québec (Province)
I. Feldstein, Peter, 1962– II. Title.
HQ117.D6713 2005   306.74'3   C2005–901187-4

This book was typeset by Interscript Inc. in 11/15 Sabon.

Contents

Foreword

One may be for or against prostitution, one may adhere to an ideology that seeks to abolish, regulate, or normalize it (through decriminalization or legalization, for example), but one cannot deny its existence all around us. Prostitution by women and children of both sexes has been much in the spotlight in recent years; child prostitution has become a particularly disturbing international industry with multiple ramifications including sex tourism, pornography, and slavery. Meanwhile, adult male prostitution has tended to remain in the shadows. The great majority of it takes place between men within a world and a context that resist feminist analysis of patriarchal domination, the theoretical structure most often used to explain the imposition of sexuality, or even sexual slavery, upon women and children. This book is intended as neither a critique of nor an apology for male prostitution or sex work (we use the terms indiscriminately). It simply seeks to dissipate the clouds of mystery

surrounding it. In this effort we rely on the personal accounts of those who practise this profession – for a profession indeed it is, at least in their eyes. Nevertheless, it
is unique among professions in at least two important
respects: no formal training is offered, and no social
protection is provided.

Since John Schlessinger's 1969 film *Midnight Cowboy*
first brought the subject into the public eye, male prostitution and sex work in general have diversified and expanded. Like the character played by Jon Voight, today's
"rent boys" are seeking adventure and, especially, ready
cash, but they find themselves in an activity in which
idealism and disillusion lock horns. Though they may
lack the features and physique of cult film idols, they
have learned to act as if they possessed them. In fact, the
male prostitution market is a universe shot through with
illusions. Fantasy reigns supreme, whether deliberately
cultivated by sex workers to entice their clients or pro-
jected by clients onto the young men whose services they
hire. And there is more than just human interest in the
life stories and analysis contained in this work: there is
psychological, sociological, and anthropological interest, for perhaps nothing so reveals a society or culture as
its sexuality, particularly the clandestine, furtive aspects
of it.

This work is certainly not free of interpretation and
conjecture, but it has no pre-set agenda other than to be
attentive to what we saw and heard. We simply considered it important to listen to and understand the men

whose profession requires them to have sex with other men while, in many cases, ignoring their own desires. We were also obstinately determined to transcend clichés by pushing our analysis beyond mere description. In short, we sought to develop models that could serve to analyze the complex reality of rent boys.

RENT BOYS

1

Background to the Study

Social science research projects, like the people they study, have multi-stranded histories, and this one is no exception. It began as a Health Canada grant application to elucidate the strategies of young sex workers vis-à-vis human immunodeficiency virus (HIV) transmission, among other issues. However, it also represented a continuation of a fifteen-year-old book, *Les enfants de la prostitution*,[1] in which my colleague Denis Ménard and I, then front-line social workers, attempted to shed light on a largely clandestine phenomenon: child and teenage prostitution, by boys in particular. In this book I pick up the story of that age group where we left it, at the threshold of adulthood. The respondents in this study averaged about twenty years of age at the time of their entrance into full-time prostitution.

In truth, my interest in these matters dates back to when, as a child living in a disadvantaged neighbourhood of Montreal, I regularly crossed paths with prostitutes of both sexes, little understanding who they were or what they were about. The subject was taboo, especially for a child, yet the sex workers themselves were visible. Montreal's downtown red-light district was famous for its brothels, most of them specializing in young women but some offering men. With the city less than an hour's drive from the United States border, Americans as well as Canadians apparently travelled great distances to visit this "tourist attraction." In the early 1960s a young Mayor Jean Drapeau launched a "war on prostitution" that did little to eliminate the phenomenon, although it did put an end to the brothel system for all practical purposes. The prostitution map was redrawn, with the street becoming the prime locus of solicitation, and escort agencies and strip clubs taking over the vacant niche of the indoor sex trade.

For the purposes of this book, we define sex work or prostitution as any activity consisting in the provision of sexual services solely or primarily for remuneration. In this study my research team[2] and I focused on what are, to our knowledge, the three most common types of sex work among North American men today: street hustling, the best known and most visible type; stripping, which takes place in specialized bars and often (as we shall see) involves an offering of "extras"; and escorting, in which high-priced sexual services are offered indirectly through an agency or other organized channel. Our recruitment of respondents concentrated on young men who currently or until recently engaged in these activities on a part- or full-time basis.

We restricted our study group to men because their status is more obscure than that of female sex workers but also, according to the professionals (doctors, nurses, social workers, and street workers in particular) who work with them, because their ways of coping with the risks of sexually transmitted disease (STD) and human immunodeficiency virus (HIV) infection are especially worrisome. In our estimation these issues have not received much attention, much less formal study by social scientists.

There was no easy way to contact young sex workers for such a project. Especially at the beginning we drew on the valuable cooperation of Projet Intervention Prostitution de Québec (PIPQ), one of the oldest community organizations working with these young people in the province. PIPQ's street workers steered us away from many pitfalls, enriched our knowledge, and initiated us in the *modus vivendi* of prostitutes. Our interviewers, Ginette Paré and Olivier Charron in Quebec City and Patrick Berthiaume in Montreal, had to show creativity and at times temerity in order to gain access to a world in which those who ask questions are regarded with extreme distrust, a world highly impermeable to even the best-trained, best-intentioned young researchers. For each interview granted, they met with numerous refusals. This said, it would be unjust to exclude mention of the many respondents who welcomed our efforts with enthusiasm, persuaded by our open-ended questions, our attentiveness to their accounts, and our relaxed interviewing style that our interest in them was of a different nature than what they are used to.

In gaining sex workers' cooperation, we had to overcome two hurdles. The first was that we did not represent an especially high-paying contract. We paid twenty dollars for a one-hour interview, generally less than they could earn elsewhere. The second was that we were asking them for a privileged look into an intimate part of their lives, to emerge, however briefly, from the clandestinity of prostitution, and to trust us in an industry where trust is a rare commodity.

Male sex workers, as they themselves attest, face a myriad of prejudices and stereotypes, and we hope that our small study will go some distance in challenging them. We ask the reader to listen to these young men's stories without preconceived attitudes and to give due consideration to our analysis, for we feel that giving a voice to the voiceless is one of the essential duties of every social sciences researcher.

Our Health Canada funding required us to focus initially on young sex workers' STD and HIV prevention strategies. We quickly realized that their attitudes towards risk would remain largely opaque to us unless we inquired into their personal and family backgrounds, their modes of entry into and operation within sex work, and their habitual practices with clients. We would also have to learn about their images of themselves and their clients as well as their negotiating skills. Put simply, we had to answer the following question: How does one become and – more importantly – remain a sex worker? Our project quickly overflowed the narrow confines imposed by our initial research question, for it seemed impossible to apprehend commercial sexual behaviour, whatever the level of risk involved, without a prior understanding of its practitioners' motivations.

Consequently, our raw material consisted of careful but discreet observation of the relevant social environments and, especially, an analysis of the personal accounts of our respondents. We asked them to describe what may be termed their "sexual career": the succession of events, practices, and relations constituting their lifelong sexual experience. These testimonials were gathered by means of semi-directed interviews consisting of a series of open questions, for example, "Tell me how ..." Our analysis of the interviews highlights both the similarities and differences among the respondents, the similarities pointing to a degree of unity in the phenomenon under study, the differences serving to identify different or even diametrically opposed life patterns.

The outline of this book is as follows: Having specified our research objectives and methods, we proceed in chapter 2 to discuss the principal personal characteristics of the study respondents. Chapter 3, "Male Prostitution Front and Centre," introduces the actors on this stage and elucidates the interests they defend. In chapter 4 we examine the conditions under which various types of sex work are practised. This discussion is followed in chapters 5 and 6 by an analysis of four typical life patterns or profiles we discerned among the respondents, our goal being to encapsulate the varying approaches of rent boys to their trade. Chapter 7 elucidates the contrasts and similarities among these patterns. In chapter 8, "Risks of the

Trade," we consider these young men's health and safety concerns as well as their strategies for coping with the dangers inherent in their work (especially STD and HIV transmission). Chapter 9, "When They Need Help," presents several suggestions for people in the helping professions and others whose work brings them into contact with these young men. The work concludes with an author's afterword, a more personal rendering in which certain as yet unanswered questions are considered.

2

Our Respondents

We considerably underestimated the challenges involved in recruiting young men for a sex work survey. Many of those approached either declined to participate or did not show up for the interview, even though the time and place had been clearly agreed upon. Potential respondents among street hustlers were more accessible than strippers and escorts, thanks in part to the cooperation of experienced street workers. Strip clubs and escort agencies were singularly unresponsive. One club owner did become receptive after ascertaining the purpose of our work, and we secured the collaboration of two escort agency managers, one at the outset and a second towards the end of the study.

In total, forty young men who met our definition of sex worker agreed to be interviewed. To come within the definition, they had to have worked or be currently working on a regular basis in street or bar prostitution, or "hustling" (nearly three-fourths of the respondents), stripping (more than one-fourth of the respondents), or escorting (more than one-third of the respondents). These young men often travelled extensively from city to city in both Canada and the United States and had worked variously in Montreal, Quebec City, and other large cities. As well as engaging in one or more of the above activities, at least one respondent had practised erotic massage, while another had acted in Los Angeles in pornographic videos nominally directed at a homosexual clientele.

The average age of the respondents when they began sex work on a regular basis was about twenty, and they had all done so either in adolescence or adulthood. At the time of the interview their average age was twenty-seven. Seventeen described themselves as homosexual, thirteen as heterosexual, and ten as more or less bisexual. The average age of first voluntary sexual relations was thirteen to fifteen, earlier than for the general male population. More than half the respondents had been victims of sexual abuse by a father, mother, mother's boyfriend, older cousin, priest, child-care worker, babysitter, uncle, neighbour, family friend, foster parent, or youth centre worker, and in some cases by more than one person. Some hesitated to define what they had endured as abuse. This was evident, for instance, in their evasive language when describing their undesired "initiation" into sex at age nine or ten by a cousin or babysitter, or the obligation to participate in their parents' sexual activity at age five or six. Some simply declined to answer the question "so as not to hurt anybody" – in itself a suggestive response.

The proportion of sexual assault victims among the respondents is overwhelmingly greater than the estimated figure of 16 per cent for boys in North America, exceeding it by a factor of 3.5 to 4 and perhaps more.[3] The secrecy, silence, and forced sexuality experienced by many respondents undoubtedly affected their subsequent life trajectory. Furthermore, two respondents were raped so savagely by "clients" at the start of their careers that they had to be hospitalized. In short, many respondents had experienced physical and sexual abuse both before and during their years of prostitution.

It is evident from the profiles of our respondents that many experienced serious relational problems with their parents at an early age, whether a rejecting and violent father or a mother indifferent to their needs. Many had to be placed in foster homes or put up for adoption. Their experiences in these substitute environments were not generally positive, and their initial contact with prostitution occurred, in many cases, when they ran away from home (at as early as age eleven).

Both urban and rural origins were well represented, while children from poorer socioeconomic backgrounds were disproportionately numerous. The fact that some respondents had to help supplement the family income by finding a job partially explains the low average level of schooling; only six respondents attended post-secondary institutions, while the majority dropped out in their mid-teens and some much earlier at eleven or twelve. Only two respondents attended university, but neither obtained a degree.

Several of the respondents currently have or once had a stable partner, and nearly one-fourth (nine) have one or more children, though not all have custody or even regular contact. A considerably larger number perceive themselves as solitary or in search of one-night stands or "fuck friends" – acquaintances with whom they can have sex without emotional commitment.

Five respondents disclosed that they are HIV-positive or living with AIDS, but several did not know their status, so this figure must be treated as approximate. Other health problems, largely linked to malnutrition or substance abuse, plague the street hustlers and some of our other respondents.

Finally, the majority were working or had previously worked "as boys," taking advantage of a juvenile and, in some cases, androgynous appearance. Only two had worked as transvestites, for a brief period.[4] However, for the majority of the youth encountered, there was no doubt that the clients were attracted by their virile appearance – accentuated, for some, by a demanding workout program. Very few reported having ever had a clientele composed mainly or exclusively of women; the clientele in nearly all cases was predominantly or exclusively male. Several respondents reported having had sex with married couples. In certain cases a "threesome" was involved, while in others the prostitute had sex with one of the partners while the other looked on.

3

Male Prostitution Front and Centre

Male prostitution has existed since ancient times. Young male prostitutes were disparaged for their lack of virility, for submitting to other men's desires passively, in the manner of women. It should of course be mentioned that the societies and cultures of the day were macho or even misogynist by today's standards. In Athens an adult male prostitute became a second-class citizen, losing all his political rights, while his clients' status remained unaffected. Child prostitution, however, was forbidden.

Contemporary historians disagree as to the importance during antiquity of sacred prostitution – that is, interceding with certain gods or goddesses by means of the sex act – but there is no doubt that it was progressively replaced by profane (remunerated) prostitution. The institution of slavery, apart from its other features, was a locus of prostitution for young people of both sexes. Their masters could do as they pleased with them; they could and did designate them as sex slaves to themselves, their sons, or other relatives. Slaves could also be confined to brothels where the master acted as a pimp.[5] In ancient Rome, boys' brothels were numerous and heavily frequented, while other youths prostituted themselves on the street, lifting their tunics to show off their genitals and entice potential clients.

Despite the abolition of slavery and, more importantly, the increasingly sharp condemnation of homosexuality by the church, male prostitution continued to prosper. According to Corinne Gauthier-Hamon and Roger Teboul,[6] young male prostitutes were not uncommon in the Middle Ages. In the larger towns many youths had few other options for survival besides begging and thieving. In the public baths that continued the tradition of the Roman *thermae* (many of them built, in fact, upon their ruins), young men offered their charms with a modicum of discretion. The tradition evidently continues to this day, especially in Europe, where certain city streets, neighbourhoods, and public parks have been known for decades or even centuries as meeting places for male clients and prostitutes.

The historian Vern L. Bullough states that male prostitution existed in the Americas well before the arrival of the European explorers.[7] It was mainly practised by persons whom the colonists termed *berdaches*,[8] or men with both masculine and feminine traits. With spreading colonization, male brothels opened in sizable towns all the way to the West Coast.[9] Apparently, cross-dressing and androgyny on the part of boys were highly prized by clients of all sexual preferences, including heterosexuals.

Prior to the emergence of the homosexual/heterosexual dichotomy in the public mind, male-to-male relations were, as in antiquity, considered acceptable from the vantage point of the active partner. (The passive partner, regarded as effeminate, may well have had a different view). As George Chauncey trenchantly puts it in *Gay New York,* the situation endured at least until the turn of the twentieth century when "the predominant form of male prostitution seems to have involved fairies selling sex to men who, despite the declaration of desire made by their willingness to pay for the encounters, identified themselves as normal."[10]

It should be said that unmarried men have frequently outnumbered available women in various contexts, particularly in developing countries and even in burgeoning North American cities. The ratio of men to women was slow to equalize in the Americas at the time of colonization and during periods of urban growth. To the great consternation of anti-prostitution (and anti-homosexual) groups, so-called "peg-houses" made their appearance. As Robin Lloyd recounts, boy prostitutes were made to sit on greased wooden pegs in order to dilate their anuses. Clients were shown the peg diameters and could choose a partner on that basis.[11]

During the Gold Rush and even earlier, brothels recruited among young male runaways, many of them penniless and in search of adventure. The promise of easy money and, later, drugs such as opium made these young men prisoners of their surroundings in short order. Of course, blackmail, coercion, and the lack of other alternatives – perhaps even a simulacrum of love on the part of their "protectors" – surely played a role. In fact, from the birth of the colonies until the present day, poor youths, finding themselves unemployed and destitute or simply unable to find female partners, have willingly prostituted themselves to men. Young sailors, soldiers, apprentices seeking a master, bodybuilders, even newsboys (in the 1900s, one-third of them carried STDs!) engaged more often than one might suppose in relations that they would probably not consider to be homosexual prostitution, but which nonetheless involved sex with men. Forced sex was also sometimes used by street gang leaders to initiate new members.[12]

In the 1940s and 1950s, male prostitution flourished even among conservative elites. It is known, for example, that a puritanical archbishop of a major American city had a penchant for young men, who were delivered to him by his chauffeur. So did J. Edgar Hoover, who was said to cross-dress when receiving male prostitutes. It is alleged that blackmail by the Mafia caused Hoover to deny this organization's existence in the United States throughout his long mandate as director of the FBI. And Senator Joseph McCarthy gained infamy as the instigator of a homosexual and communist witch hunt, yet allegedly had one-night stands with young men picked up in bars (though those close to him have always denied his homosexuality).[13] That these three stalwarts of homophobic repression were very probably involved in various types of male sex services is indicative of the hypocrisy of the American political class of that era. As for Canada – well, it is early for spectacular disclosures, and we must allow time and the historians to do their work. But this country's own history will surely one day record the secret lives of officially heterosexual politicians whose attraction to young men led them to commit imprudent acts that are generally paid for in cash or drugs. Let us be even more categorical: the world over and through the ages, wherever and whenever men (or at times women) of power and fortune have managed to induce or compel young men to satisfy their sexual desires for remuneration, male prostitution has prospered.

Male prostitution, like other types of sex work, may be conceptualized as a *mise en scène* of four different groups of actors. The first group, prostitutes, share the stage with the second, their clients, the majority of them male, most coming singly but some in couples. The third group comprises all the entrepreneurs revolving around these two groups and profiting from their interaction without physically participating in it. These "sex entrepreneurs" are the proprietors of male strip clubs, escort agencies, and massage parlours as well as gay bars where young sex workers are welcomed or tolerated; the makers of pornography, who use sex workers as a raw material; drug dealers, of whom many hustlers, strippers, and their admirers are excellent clients; the operators of rooming houses, motels, and small hotels in the vicinity of places of prostitution and bars, where rooms may be rented for short periods; even general or specialized newspapers and magazines that advertise male sexual services (these advertisers are reportedly charged higher rates). The fourth group consists of individuals such as legislators, judges and, especially, opinion leaders whose mission is to produce social norms and enforce them by means of policing, prosecution, or other approaches. It is they who determine what may legally be seen in a strip show, who define the term "solicitation" for legal purposes, who determine the extent to which sites of street prostitution, strip clubs, and even escort agencies will be watched and their clients harassed. They are generally the sworn enemies of the sex entrepreneurs. In sociologist Howard Becker's terminology, they are the "moral entrepreneurs."

As Becker notes, deviance, in the sense of publicly labelled wrongdoing, is always the result of enterprise. Before any act can be viewed as deviant, and before any class of people can be labelled and treated as outsiders for committing the act, someone must have made the rule that defines the act as deviant.[14] Though prostitution between persons of legal age is not itself a crime in Canada, the following do constitute offences: communication (i.e., solicitation) for the purposes of prostitution, a provision targeting street prostitutes; procuring (pimping) and living off the income of prostitution, including the keeping of a "bawdy house"; indecency, a charge that particularly affects strip clubs, though the case law now allows some physical contact in private booths; and corruption of morals, including the pornography provisions. From the societal standpoint, then, prostitution offers various points of entry into

deviance and delinquency even though it is not an of-
fence as such. This ambiguity is not without impact on
the daily lives of sex workers.

It seems clear that our difficulty in finding respondents
for our study was in part due to sex workers' fears of being judged, lectured to, tracked, or entrapped under the
laws and regulations that limit or punish their activities.
Such distrust is even more understandable when one realizes that many sex workers have had run-ins with the police and/or the courts as a direct or an indirect (for
example, drug or theft cases) result of prostitution.

It is true, of course, that sex workers are not the only
ones who expose themselves to prosecution under the
prostitution laws of Canada and most U.S. states. Clients and sex entrepreneurs too can be charged with solicitation or keeping a bawdy house, living off the income
of prostitution, or producing, distributing, or possessing
pornography. Nevertheless, sex workers bear the brunt
of punitive action. Not only do they carry on their shoul-
ders an incommensurate responsibility but they essentially shield clients and sex entrepreneurs with their own
bodies, allowing them to profit from sex work and preserve their invisibility at the same time. Nor should one
overlook the interests of the "moral entrepreneurs," an
odd-seeming category that is nonetheless decisive in the
definition of prostitution as a social problem.

The clients represent the hidden face of prostitution.
As our respondents told us, "regular" or familiar clients
are not in the majority, and thus many of them are
strangers even to the prostitutes. Clients are described

as being of any age, appearance, sexual orientation or
identity, of having all manner of preferences and tastes.
Nonetheless, many respondents expressed their continual surprise at the number of recently married men
("When you see the baby seat in the back of the car,
you understand a lot of things!" one commented) as
well as divorced men coping with their homosexuality
or bisexuality. These men's need for anonymity and
clandestinity is evidently satisfied by secretive contact
with a rent boy.

It may seem surprising that so many clients claim to be
heterosexual even as they pay young men for sex. But if
sexual orientation is, as seems clear, only a matter of
self-labelling, then one understands why many men may
not see this state of affairs as a contradiction. They can
keep their homosexual relations a secret, partitioning
them off from the emotional involvements that charac-
terize the rest of their life. They may regard paying a sex
worker as offering themselves a service rather than having a same-sex relationship. Indeed, as Canadian researcher Barry Adam and his team at the University of
Windsor have showed, self-definition as homosexual,
gay, or bisexual has more to do with same-sex emotional
involvement than with sexuality as such.[15] Moreover, in
prostitution, money not only imposes a symbolic distance between individuals; it establishes a power relationship in which the prostitute tends to be objectified. It
is not, generally speaking, a relationship of reciprocal
desire and pleasure but an instrumentalized one, in the
sense that the sex worker's role is to be a pleasure pro-

vider for the paying client. The client's erotic identity need never be an issue, and for many clients this is exactly as it should be. This explains their demand for absolute secrecy; they do not see their escapades in the world of prostitution as having anything to do with their "real" lives.

Intimacy and virility are what the client requires and buys – or rents, rather, for a few moments or a whole night. If the system manages to serve its purpose so well, it is largely because North Americans have sacralized and at times associated these two virtues. Male prostitution is driven by this association between the intimacy that so many men of all sexual orientations find nowhere but in sex, and the virility that is idealized to such an extent that anyone who believes he lacks it will seek it in another man. It is also possible that the porno video and magazine market has inculcated in clients an expectation of certain images and fantasies; hence the young hunk, muscles rippling from bodybuilding, heterosexual in appearance even though he has sex with other men.

Our respondents tended to dichotomize their clients: the young versus the old, the "nice guys" versus the "assholes," the regular versus the occasional, the ones looking for a good listener versus the ones who want as much sex as possible for their money. As we might guess, younger clients are generally preferred to older ones, nice guys more respected than assholes, regulars less anxiety-provoking than strangers, emotional ones more appreciated than the sex-obsessed. Thus clients, like prostitutes (as we shall see in more detail), fall within a hierarchy.

The conventional wisdom that pimps and gangs are uncommon in adult male prostitution seems accurate, especially by comparison with the situation of female sex workers and even underage boys. To be sure, the kind of gross subjugation or slavery affecting young boys is rarely found with older males; yet this does not mean the men are free of submission or dependency or that no one makes money off of them. In fact, a host of sex entrepreneurs revolves around male prostitutes, seeking to siphon off some of their substantial incomes and those of their clients. Like other researchers before us, we repeatedly heard that the world of male prostitution is largely under the influence of organized crime. This is probably the case for the many drug dealers doing brisk business with these men, the escort agencies, massage parlours, and strip clubs employing them, and the bars allowing them to solicit clients. However, confirmation of this hypothesis was far beyond the scope of our research, and would not be straightforward in any case, for the subject is controversial even among veteran police officers and street workers. But there is money being made, of that we can be certain; if there were not, these services would not exist. Like any lucrative market, male prostitution is driven by the laws of supply and demand.

Moreover, we were surprised at the extent of self-policing in the sex trade. Strippers, for example, cannot do as they please with clients, and if they disobey certain unwritten rules, serious consequences can ensue. Monitors intervene between the parties if there is sexual touching or drug-taking in public, telling them that things have gone too far. In bars the dictates of discretion apparently keep solicitation by sex workers under wraps. Drug dealers, of course, are discreet in the extreme; only insiders know who they are and how to buy from them without attracting suspicion or getting kicked out of a bar. Everyone's interest is in protecting illicit business by keeping it out of sight.

As to the moral entrepreneurs, their role may be low or high profile; from time to time, depending on the social and political conjuncture, it may receive extensive media coverage. Public demonstrations and police raids momentarily make noise and interfere with business, but then calm follows the storm. The whole industry operates as if there were a delicate balance to be maintained between public morals and public opinion. Thus, what is tolerated in one city or neighbourhood may not survive public outrage in another. Certain streets and bars appear to be under particularly high surveillance, and places of prostitution may therefore migrate not only seasonally but also in response to the hazards run by sex workers, clients, and sex entrepreneurs.

In reality, it is not just the moral entrepreneurs who have their eyes on sex work – everyone involved is watching one another. Sex workers have to attract clients legally while avoiding solicitation or indecency charges, so they keep a low profile with respect to police and local residents. Clients clearly put a premium on discretion, avoiding contact with the law to the extent that their very existence may be overlooked.

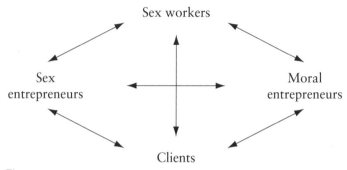

Figure 1

Meanwhile, the sex entrepreneurs have to keep their business running smoothly, keeping at bay those (such as "problem" clients, police, or moral entrepreneurs) who would pry too assiduously.

Which of these people is right or wrong is of no relevance here; in justifying their actions, they all invoke motives they see as legitimate. The important observation is that sex work takes place within a network of competing interests, tensions, and oppositions and cannot be studied in isolation from them. Figure 1 illustrates these interactions, showing that sex workers are far from alone on the stage of male prostitution.

This figure reminds us that the four groups involved in male prostitution are actors in a drama whose denouement cannot be determined by any one group alone; rather, it depends on the interactions among them. Each party's actions have inevitable repercussions for the others. During periods of more relaxed public morality, bar owners adapt accordingly, and "contact dances" in private booths, involving sexual touching between sex workers and clients, make their appearance, as they now have in Canada. When citizens rise up against visible street prostitution and moral entrepreneurs go into action, sex workers and clients observe discretion, change their tactics, or move to a new area. Prices fluctuate according to the supply of sexual services (number of prostitutes) and the demand for same (number of clients), not to mention the availability of certain drugs prized by both parties.

In summary, male prostitution may appear at first sight as a relatively free market, but it is in fact regulated and controlled from within (mainly by the sex entrepreneurs) and without (by the moral entrepreneurs). As the sociologist François Delor pertinently wrote, "sexual interaction between a young prostitute and his client takes place within a context of power relations based on economic or symbolic domination, which the two partners cannot alter by their own actions."[16] There are too many people and interests at play around them.

4

Working Conditions

All forms of sex work – street hustling, stripping, escorting – are trades learned by contact or apprenticeship with more experienced individuals, for example, family members, peers, or clients. None of these activities has any place in our formal educational system.[17] This apprenticeship is a difficult process of trial and error: clients may behave unpredictably, contact with moral entrepreneurs must be minimized, and sex entrepreneurs may require placating. As we shall see in this chapter, rent boys' apprenticeship is made more difficult by the complex codes of conduct specific to each type of sex work. Young men who do not master them cannot even begin, much less continue, to practise this activity.

Street hustling usually takes place on a block known to be conducive to quick meetings between clients and prostitutes. It may also occur in bars or peep shows,[18] especially on winter nights when the sidewalks are less welcoming. These places are mostly located close to businesses with a homosexual clientele – restaurants or taverns, for example – or strip clubs. A notable exception is that of certain shopping centres and parks which, although frequented by the general public, are known as sites where the youngest prostitutes in particular are to be found. Several respondents met their first clients there as teenagers.

The respondents consider street hustling to be "the bottom rung of the ladder" because it is generally poorly paid and more dangerous. The hustler is likely to be arrested for solicitation, robbed or raped by clients, or hounded out of a territory by other sex workers or their protectors. Nevertheless, some respondents had no ambition other than hustling, despite the hazards. One commented: "At the start there were a few of us, we were friends. But as soon as I was out on the street I would go off with a client. The other guys didn't like that, the way the clients ran after me. The other guys on the street threatened to break both my legs, bust my face, or rip my head off."

Another recounted: "Clients are brutal with me at times, especially the big tough ones. They get violent when I suck them off. They hold my head and jam their dick down my throat until I choke. When I have anal sex, some of them try to hurt me on purpose, as if they wanted to bust me open."

How do clients recognize street hustlers? They are young men who can be seen waiting at known locations for other prostitutes and for clients at certain hours, especially after dark. They are easily identifiable with practice by the way they lope along the sidewalk trying to entice potential clients: "It's all in the body, the attitude, the posture, especially the look in your eye," said one youth, and several of his peers concurred. For others, the clothing and what it suggests count for a great deal. Clothes advertise a personality type likely to please certain types of clients – ideally, the largest possible number.

The prices charged by street hustlers vary greatly according to the sex act requested and the amount of time it takes. Mutual masturbation costs less than oral sex, which costs less than anal sex or "extras" such as sadomasochistic relations. Other factors include the time of year, the volume of clients, the hustler's immediate needs, and the client's attractiveness. Prices generally range from $20 to $60 for a briefly performed sex act. Strippers and escorts generally charge much more – $150 to $200 and upwards, but escorts will spend more time and allow more elaborate sexual activity.

The hustler's typical client is usually a motorist (occasionally a pedestrian) who circles the block several times, assessing his options, stopping to negotiate practices and prices and leaving if none of the young men is to his liking. Some of our respondents explained that caution is in order because undercover police may also display this behaviour. Masturbation or fellatio usually takes place in the client's car. If more space and time is needed, the pair will go to a sauna, rooming house, or small hotel, or more rarely to the client's or young man's home. This latter option is generally reserved for regular clients in whom the sex worker has developed a minimum of trust. Hustlers will occasionally venture into larger hotels to attract travelling businessmen, some of them apparently quite wealthy, but they point out that "you have to have short hair, wear nice clothes, be really clean, and sit there like you're part of the furniture. If it works, pretty soon you're invited for a drink, and then it winds up a little later in a room upstairs."

Experienced hustlers who meet clients in private rooms always make sure the client undresses first, so as to examine his body ("Does he look like he might have any diseases?") but also to avoid falling into a police dragnet. In general, they ask the client to put the money on the night table in advance so as to avoid any misunderstandings.

Unlike the street, the strip club is an enclosed space in which the unsaid is omnipresent and the interplay of gazes and glances is sovereign. Such establishments generally open for business in the evening and stay open until three A.M. A bouncer, usher, or manager discreetly controls clients' and strippers' comings and goings. Strippers are paid a minimal base wage for their stage show and earn extra income by offering various services. The show is presented on a central stage around which the clients' tables and chairs are arranged. In general, the show is divided into two parts. First, the stripper begins to undress to rhythmic music, baring his torso or somewhat more. He then performs a slower, more lascivious dance to a ballad, undressing completely or almost. What exactly is shown on stage in any instance depends on the rules of the bar, the city where it is located, and the dancer's comfort level.

This public spectacle by the strippers, each in turn, is in fact designed for the sole purpose of enticing the client to request additional services. In the past the usual practice was for the client to invite one of the strippers to dance for him on a stool at his table, but this practice has been in decline for some time, closer proximity being now not only possible but encouraged. It takes place in small, dimly lit rooms at a certain remove from the main bar area. The most common of these – one might almost say traditional – is a semi-private room where the stripper moves the stool closer to the client (between his spread legs, in fact) and dances for the length of one song. The standard "five-dollar" dance (though it may cost six or more) done here resembles the stage routine, offering a closer view but minimal physical contact. More popular dances costing ten dollars, twenty dollars, or more allow mutual touching and fondling. Surveillance is claimed to be vigilant so as to prevent acts such as genital fondling or fellatio that are illegal in public, but the reality is that the darkness of the room, the amounts of money changing hands, and the guard's arbitrary judgment militate in favour of more relaxed enforcement. A recent development is a second, totally private type of room in which erotic activities can go further: fellatio, mutual masturbation, or more, depending on the client's willingness to spend. Surveillance is nearly impossible. This option is now offered by most strip clubs in Canada, and its popularity is on the rise.

The stripper tries to boost the client's excitement to an increasingly high pitch from song to song, gaining his loyalty so as to maximize the total earnings. The more expensive dance options are not posted in the bar; rather, clients, if not in the know, are discreetly informed by the stripper of their existence. The stripper might suggest, for instance, that "a special client like yourself" may be interested in the possibility of more intimate activities. The client's bill can easily mount into the hundreds of dollars in an evening if the stripper accompanies him home or to a hotel at the end of the night. Several strippers said that they regularly do such "overtime." The negotiated price will depend on the stripper's popularity, the client's apparent wealth, the sex acts requested, and the time required. One youth commented: "The better looking the stripper is, the better shape he's in, the more demanding he'll be and the higher the price he can charge for extras if he does overtime with a client." Some strippers admit that "after hours" is when their job really becomes profitable, but most prefer to avoid the subject; no stripper wishes to look like a common hustler in the eyes of his peers. In the sex-work hierarchy, strippers assiduously preserve their status, especially if they claim to be heterosexual: "The subject of overtime is taboo. Nobody tells anybody. No stripper will say that he turns tricks, not even me, and I do. Nobody wants to be taken for a hustler. The guys want to preserve their male image."

It is a kind of irony that the hyper-masculine image that strippers must uphold in order to seduce clients makes them reticent to admit any involvement in prostitution. They tend to say that their being or passing for heterosexual (or perhaps bisexual) excites some clients who glimpse the possibility of violating yet another taboo – introducing a young heterosexual to homosexual passion. Some clients' goal does appear to be just that: to possess (or have the impression of possessing) the idealized, inaccessible, virile, heterosexual young man of their fantasies.

Even though most strippers have sex for pay on an occasional or regular basis, silence reigns on the topic. The frequently fierce competition among them generally keeps them from confiding in their peers. As well, the ideal for many strippers, especially those who are homosexual or bisexual, is to find one or, better yet, several "sugar daddies," older, well-off lovers willing to support them financially, buying them cars, trips, drugs, or jewelry or setting them up in an apartment. Such men being in short supply, they are jealously guarded.

Strippers broadly classify clients into two types: "dirty old men," described as "not mean but sometimes aggressive; they try to fondle you as much as they can," and "teddy bears," who have "more of a need to talk than to touch. They mainly come to tell you about their problems, they're looking for company." However, one respondent nuances this dichotomy: "Clients, you eventually figure out that what they're doing is looking for sex to get affection. There are exceptions, but in general what they're really after is affection."

It is no exaggeration to say that strippers watch their clients as much as their clients watch them. Most strippers consider their own attractiveness to be a function of their gaze as well as their physique. They explained to us that very careful observation of clients in the room is required to detect those who appear to be interested in them or their bodies:

> I observe the clients. I observe the ones who are watching me. I observe how they're dressed, how they walk, how they hold their glass. I analyze them from A to Z. I especially try to figure out if they're interested in me or not, if they have money. I give myself five minutes and then I go over to them. You have to find something to talk about. If you want to make money with a client, you can't go on about your own problems ... You have to talk about things that interest him, you have to figure out what interests him, you need enough vocabulary and culture to carry on a conversation. If the client runs out of things to say after five minutes, there's no point staying there. If you offer him a dance in the back [in a private booth] and he declines, then he didn't come for you ... Maybe another guy will have a better chance, somebody more his type. Sometimes we'll signal to each other. But you can't waste time. The reason why I'm there is to make money.

Yet some strippers remain aloof, odd though this strategy may seem: "I don't really approach the clients. I wait for them to come over to me. I do my dance on the stage and then I walk around the room a bit. That's it. If someone talks to me or offers me a drink, I'll go see him, I'll agree to dance for him, get acquainted. But rarely will I approach clients myself."

We turn now to escorting, which consists of a more or less explicit but indirect offering of high-priced sexual services. Some escorts describe their anatomy in minute detail, others are allusive. These encounters are generally though not always mediated by an agency whose function is not only to make appointments and manage the business but also to provide a degree of protection for the sex worker. Freelance escorts, however, also exist. The worker's contact number (usually a cell phone) is advertised in newspapers or, more recently, on the Internet. In agencies, a wide range of physical types is advertised with facial photos, and every possible and imaginable "extra" is available – for the right price, of course. A driver/bodyguard delivers and picks up the escort, knows the whereabouts of the two parties and the length of their engagement, and can intervene in the rare event that the worker's safety is threatened. For these services the agency generally takes a commission of half the escort's earnings. In all these respects, the organization of the male escort trade does not differ much from that of its female counterpart.

Several respondents who are self-employed male escorts claim that this status is more common than among female escorts. The ads for these freelance sex workers tend to show part of their anatomy but not their face. Yet another arrangement is a kind of partnership among two or three escorts who share the cost of advertising, rent, and other expenses.

As one might expect, nights and evenings are the peak business hours for all escorts. The usual meeting place with the client is at a hotel, motel, or sauna. Some clients may invite them home, while some self-employed escorts will allow clients, especially regulars, to come to their own homes. Most escorts – whether they are self-employed, working for an agency, or both (although the agencies formally demand exclusivity) – perceive their activities as a business. Escorts are the group of male sex workers who charge the highest rates and enjoy the highest status. They also have the most female clients, generally businesswomen or the spouses of well-to-do or well-known – but frequently absent – men.

To sum up the discussion so far, our respondents' remarks indicate that male sex work takes place on three relatively distinct levels: escorts at the top of the hierarchy; strippers, whose status varies according to their popularity at any given time; and street hustlers, looked down upon by the other two groups and by society at large. There is some mobility and overlap among the groups; some strippers, for example, also work as escorts. More significantly, the merciless reality of the male prostitution market dictates that popularity waxes and wanes as a function of ephemeral traits such as youth, beauty, and physical fitness. Therefore, mobility tends to be downward with age.

5

Four Life Patterns

Our analysis of the forty accounts gathered led us to identify four typical life patterns among young sex workers, which we describe succinctly below. The criteria we used in determining these patterns include sex workers' feelings and impressions, their images of self and clients, and their mode of entry into the profession. In chapter 6, each of these patterns is illustrated by a relatively typical case.

Slightly over half of our respondents (twenty-two) fall within a group we shall term the *Outcasts*. Many of them live in a situation that can fairly be called dire poverty (only one had another, low-paying job). They are surviving day to day with little chance to dream of the future: "My reason to live? I haven't found it yet." This sex-work pattern is so markedly characterized by substance abuse that it can be difficult to determine for any individual whether the habit engendered the career or vice versa. Most Outcasts use the money they earn from hustling to buy alcohol and drugs, and many are grappling with serious addictions. The vast majority use alcohol and especially hard drugs before, during, or after their encounters with clients. "The money I made didn't go into the bank: it went up my nose!" said one respondent with a laugh. Cocaine, heroin, and, in truth, any mind-altering substance has a good chance of winding up in their hands and then their bodies. With one exception, this was the only group that included intravenous drug users, at least half of the respondents stating this behaviour; it was also the group comprising all confirmed cases of HIV transmission. These respondents were the earliest entrants into the sex trade, half of them before the age of sixteen. The youngest began at age eleven, the oldest at about thirty, for an average age of eighteen.

Self-esteem among the Outcasts is very low, their despair palpable. Their sojourn in prostitution is most often the sequel to a painful childhood. Many ran away from home to escape physical or sexual violence, but their subsequent trajectory has only deepened their negative image of self and others:

For the clients my body is an object, a piece of meat. It's very hard on my self-esteem.

I see myself as a garbage can that's been soiled, washed, bleached, but it's still dirty, especially since I got HIV from doing this.

As the years go by, your emotional, psychological, and sexual problems build up. You can't imagine the degrading, humiliating things clients can do to you ... it messes up a lot of things in your life afterward.

Nearly all of these men (twenty out of twenty-two) were or had previously been street hustling on a regular (in most cases daily) basis; only a few had worked at any time in stripping or escorting. Some had received prison sentences for theft or other drug-related crimes. Nearly all had unhappy childhoods or teen years. Many had been in a series of foster families or homes, and their natural or substitute parents were negligent or rejecting, especially if the boys came out as homosexuals. Criminal, incestuous, alcoholic and violent behaviours were common. The immediate precursor to prostitution for many was dropping out of school, running away from home, and finding themselves trying to survive on the street.

This group also included the largest number of sexual abuse victims. Most were repeatedly victimized during childhood or early adolescence. In prostitution they relive one of the gravest of childhood traumas: secretive, guilt-ridden, non-reciprocal sexual relations. Some of these emotionally deprived young men spoke of prostitution as a quest for attention or affection, cost what it may: "I learned that to get affection, you have to give sex." They are largely solitary individuals who have rarely experienced continuous or stable friendships or love relationships.

The other half of the respondents could be divided equally among the three other patterns (six respondents each). It should be said that these four patterns are not mutually exclusive; some of the respondents have experienced more than one. Still, one pattern usually predominated, and we grouped the respondents on that basis.

Part-Timers is our term for young men who opt for sporadic sex work primarily to "make ends meet" – to supplement their income and pay off debts such as student or car loans. It enables them to add undeclared income to their social assistance or unemployment benefits, or afford luxuries that would otherwise be beyond their means. Heavy drug or alcohol use is rare in this group and is more or less absent as a motivating factor.

The Part-Timers are the group who began sex work the latest: between ages twenty-two and forty, for an average age of about twenty-eight years. They are comparatively well educated among our respondents, suggesting an important reason why they generally consider the job a sideline, occasional gig, or stopping point on the road to a better (if hypothetical) occupation. Thus, one respondent compared his situation to that of any other self-employed worker. Only one of these men hustled on the street; the others were strippers if heterosexual, escorts if homosexual. Another of their characteristics is that they do not really identify with sex work, always perceiving it as accessory to their lives. Several are married with children and have what they see as a "real" though temporary or insufficiently paid job. For all these reasons their sex work is generally discreet, undisclosed to family and friends. Despite their initial apprehensions, they may come to derive a degree of self-affirmation from prostitution, if, for example, it enables them to meet people of a certain social or intellectual status. They tend to be proud of staying sober and in control while on the job.

Insiders, in our terminology, are young men who have grown up in or around the sex trade to the point that they come to view it as their primary social circle, their "family." They may have been encouraged by their families of origin – a mother working as a prostitute, for example – or forced to find a support network while very young. Some were thrown out of the house when their homosexuality was discovered; others moved from one foster family to another without forming any durable bonds. In some cases they were recruited into sex work by friends already involved in prostitution. As a result, these boys began sex work early, at an average age of seventeen (fifteen to twenty-one). However, their motivations are completely different from those of the Outcasts. They do not regard sex work as a desperate resort but as something natural, an honourable living, despite the hazards associated with it: "All my friends, all the guys I used to hang out with in gay circles, they were all prostitutes. The first guy I loved was a hustler. One day he brought me a client of his, a tourist, who wanted to get to know me. The guy was cool, he was nice. After that it basically became a routine. It's also a kind of attraction. How can I put it? Prostitution is like a drug. I enjoy it."

All the Insiders use alcohol and drugs to varying degrees. Some have tried "other things" as occupations but returned to the sex trade because they missed it. "The street is the only place I know where I feel at home," said one. "Your friends are there, it becomes like a family. You're never alone." Said another, "It's like an adrenalin rush. It's a great feeling to know that the street is yours, it's your playground, it's a part of your life." These young men give a greater impression of positive socialization than the Outcasts. Most have had relatively stable friendships and love relationships. Nearly all hustle on the street or did so in the past, but half of them subsequently went into stripping or escorting.

We use the term *Liberationists* to describe young homosexuals (except for one man who defined himself as an "exhibitionist heterosexual") for whom prostitution is a way of living out fantasies, exploring new experiences and partners, and profiting from these discoveries. Their age of entry into the trade is highly variable, from sixteen to thirty, for an average of about twenty years. The majority of these men did not experience severe problems during childhood; they maintain good if distant contact with their families. They have higher levels of education than their colleagues. Unlike the Outcasts, the Liberationists exhibit high self-esteem and an overall positive outlook on their activities and clients: they like what they do. They may develop emotional bonds with certain clients. All of them state that they chose the sex trade for the many personal and relational advantages it offers, such as the opportunity to meet a "sugar daddy." In short, they see their work first and foremost as an

opportunity to affirm their sexual orientation or prefer-
ence and to grow as an individual. One explained, "I
went to a strip club and it looked like fun. I was attracted to it. I thought the guys were lucky to be doing
it. At the time I didn't accept myself as gay; it was a way
for me to become gay and happy as well."

Since their occupation fills part of their needs, love relationships for these men are often casual or long distance. One senses here a rebellion of sorts against
"traditional" values; sex work, for the Liberationists, is
a way to be "not like everybody else." For some, it is
also a kind of social work. They stress the human side of
their encounters with clients, some of whom depend on
such contact for their emotional health. Drug-taking in
this group is generally limited to marijuana or alcohol.

The drawback to this apparently comfortable life is
the potential for a kind of inertia to set in, hindering the
transition to other opportunities. These young men may
continue doing sex work even after their interest in it
wanes and they have learned all they feel they can.
Thus, the initial sense of liberation may morph into a
species of disillusion:

We're paid for dreams, and we wind up living in a
world of dreams ...

As time went on, I began to find it degrading, dirty,
kind of. But if I had to do it over, I would.

At first I was really happy to be an escort. It's a comfortable life, and it's pretty easy. But your brain gets

fucked up. See, it gets you material things but not necessarily pleasure. Half of the clients, I'm glad to see them, I even enjoy seeing them. They're a little in love with me, they tell me nice things. But the other half, it's just sexual, there's no communication.

Nevertheless, all the Liberationists in our study stated that the work has many positive aspects. This group challenges our preconceived notions about prostitution, its members declaring that it has the potential to be gratifying and affirming under the right circumstances and with the right clients.

6

Regular Guys

In this chapter we present four typical accounts (if such can be said to exist) illustrating each of the life patterns just described. It is important to remember that each story is only a snapshot in the life of a rent boy. Nothing binds these respondents necessarily to the pattern they displayed at the time of our interview. Moreover, at least one (Christophe) said that he had noticed an improvement in his life over the preceding weeks, reminding us that even for the Outcasts, hope is possible.

CHRISTOPHE, AN OUTCAST

Christophe is a somewhat androgynous man of twenty-one. He comes from a family of ten children with a violent and alcoholic father ("he hit me all the time, even broke some of my ribs, but we had to put up with our sickness") and a handicapped mother whose husband forced sex upon her. The seven oldest children were placed in foster families and then adopted. Christophe ran away for the first time at age eleven, shortly after an uncle sexually abused him. It was not long before he found himself on the street, looking for a way to survive. "For me," he says, "it was like a deciding factor. My uncle had abused me by force and paid me to keep my mouth shut. He was the one who introduced me to the world of sex, bars, and all that as a kid. When I became a runaway, I knew where I was going to hide, and I told myself, while you're at it, you're going to sell your ass!"

Quickly succumbing to substance abuse, Christophe nearly died of an overdose when he was sixteen. He calls it a suicide attempt: "I couldn't take feeling so awful about myself, being thought of as a garbage can, human trash, a nothing, a nobody." His vision of prostitution is starkly negative, for he has greatly suffered from it: "At first hustling seemed pretty positive, I even thought I might find love that way. But I quickly lost that illusion: if you want to hustle, you can't love yourself. It looks like an exchange of services, but basically what you are is a garbage can for society. You're stuck with people who're unable to get anything else, like married men who just want to get their rocks off, or old guys. You're immediately overcome by drugs, violence, rejection – it all comes with the territory. It's inseparable from prostitution."

At fourteen, after street hustling for several years, Christophe began to flirt with prospective clients in gay bars. He then turned towards stripping and escorting:

In bars you get them to buy you a drink, you flirt, and then you say, "Hey man, I'm commercial, and if you need my services you have to pay for them" ... At sixteen or seventeen I was an escort, first self-employed and then for an agency because I felt safer that way. You can filter the clients, and you get some protection from the agency. I was also a stripper around the same time. When you let somebody touch you, you can make quite a lot of money – and a whole lot more if you go to bed with the client later. That's what we call overtime, extras. I had very rich clients, American businessmen and famous people who I won't name. Some clients, you're like a god to them because you bring them sex, and I did everything: cross-dressing, s&m, domination with leather and whips, everything, being pissed or shat on. Because there are perverts in this business and it leaves emotional scars. The best are the ones who only want to talk. Sometimes you feel bad accepting their money because for once they're getting a human relationship. But that's rare. And then you have some regular clients with whom it's easier, because you already know what they expect from you.

For Christophe, as for most of the young men interviewed, street hustling is "the bottom rung of the ladder," whereas stripping represents a middle ground, and escorting has the highest status. Though he was well paid some weeks, Christophe admits that he always squandered his money: "Nice clothes, coke, lots of coke, colognes, aestheticians, the gym, tanning. It's crazy, but I was trying to build the same body that I was destroying with sex and drugs ... I got violent; when I was really drunk it was like, don't step on my toes, Jack. Anyway, in that occupation you have to fight to carve out a place and keep it, especially if you're in street or bar hustling"

Recently, Christophe found a boyfriend a little younger than himself. He realized that attracting the attention and love of a man his own age was not easy for him, because he found it difficult to be the hunter instead of the hunted. "I never had to turn around and pay for a guy. Still, I was lucky to find him! Because clients are not people I find physically attractive. They're forty, fifty, or sixty years old. Some of them became regulars, sugar daddies, if I may say. We saw each other from time to time, and they spoiled me a bit. They took pity on me." His new love relationship makes Christophe hopeful, and hope is something he needs: "The self-esteem I never had, I have it today because I feel loved. Maybe I'm worthy of love. But not everybody who goes through what I went through comes out alive ... "

As to STD protection, Christophe's attitude is ambiguous, to say the least. "Normally, I tell them that without a condom, no way, but for a hefty bonus ... I was lucky to never get any diseases, only crabs. Damn, do they itch, those bugs! I got AIDS tested when I did things that made me worried, like turning tricks without condoms because the guy wouldn't hear of it. You know, it's not easy to address that with them; you take your courage in hand ... Especially because I always have a few drinks first. In fact, I admit it, I'm always drunk or stoned at those times."

BILLY, A PART-TIMER

Billy's father had problems with alcoholism, while his mother sat by ineffectually. He has not seen his parents since the age of sixteen when, fed up with their bickering, he decided to move into an apartment. Since the age of twelve, he has led an active sex life with girls, including several lengthy relationships, but has always lived alone. He has joint custody of a child born to a girlfriend when he was nineteen. In his twenties, after working out extensively to develop his physique, he began working full time as a stripper in a gay bar. He also has a low-paying part-time job in a factory. His image of stripping gradually improved as time went on. "It pays pretty well," he says. "It works out to be a pretty good sideline."

The idea germinated in his mind while he was dating a female stripper:

I could see how much money she was making, whereas I had money problems, mainly debts: my car, my rent ... That's why I got started. The first night I was stressed out, even though I didn't have to get all the way undressed. It was more of a seduction show for women, and it was in another city anyway.

Because of the travel requirements, and also my kid, and the fact that women in general don't pay as well, I decided to return to Quebec City, and this is where I learned the real trade, in a gay bar. I'd never known guys who had done that job before. Girls, yeah, but not male dancers. But I set limits with my contact dances: You can touch my thighs, my torso, my ass maybe, but that's where it ends. Tough luck, bud!

Billy's integration into the world of male stripping was not an easy one: "What I found most difficult was the homo side," he says. "I've danced for women in Montreal, but men are always the biggest market for male dancers. And it's not the same atmosphere, at least not for me. With women, it's easier, all you have to do is play the seducer, whereas with men, it's more sexual, more provocative."

Billy does not take hard drugs; marijuana and alcohol suffice to get him "in the mood." However, he did have serious drug problems as a teen: "I was in four programs for that. I also dealt when I couldn't get enough to eat, but now, in the last year, I've found something much better: dancing." Since his main motive for doing the work is money, his attitude towards clients is not especially warm. "There are some okay ones who will respect you. But for others, you're like a piece of meat, they try to touch your dick, and even if I warn them they're going too far, they don't stop. I have to move away from them. The best are the ones who talk, who take you for a psychologist, practically. They just need some company. All you have to do is talk to them, almost no dancing at all. But only 15 to 20 per cent of the clients are like that."

He refuses to have sex with his clients, although like all strippers he is frequently solicited. He greatly hopes that his factory job will become permanent and full time so he can leave stripping behind. "I mean, I'm not going to be doing this forever!" he says. He also regrets that his two jobs prevent him from socializing much, going out to places where he could meet women and contemplate a stable relationship. His episodic relationships have been small consolation to him as a dancer. He does enjoy the artistic side of his routines, though, which allow him to express unexplored aspects of his personality.

At the end of the interview he admits that he has occasionally spent the night with female clients when dancing for women, perceiving them as one-night stands. He says that he always takes the necessary precautions against STDs and unwanted pregnancies, even if his partner is on the pill. "I protect myself for myself and my kid, especially now that my ex is a coke addict," he says. "Who will take care of my child if I'm not there anymore? I'm working on getting exclusive custody now." Despite his numerous lovers and his desire for stability, he is reticent to commit. "I had such a bad experience with the mother of my child," he concludes. In the end he finds it both comic and pathetic that he, a heterosexual man with a child, dances in a gay bar for other men in exactly the same situation, with spouses who have no idea what their husbands are up to.

JEAN-LOUP, AN INSIDER

Jean-Loup is a well-built, athletic man of nineteen who has been hustling full time for three years. His mother was a single parent involved in prostitution and serious substance abuse. Several of his relatives are involved in organized crime. Jean-Loup was taken from his mother very early when she was deemed incapable of parenting, and he spent his entire childhood until eighteen in a long series of foster homes and centres. He attended high school briefly before dropping out, yet he adores and writes poetry, mainly for its seductive effect on his female partners. He has stayed in touch with his mother but sees her only once or twice a year. "She's the kind of person you don't like to see too often," he says laconically. During his many placements he was often subjected to sexual touching by older boys, an occurrence he hesitates to call sexual abuse. The idea of hustling was suggested to him by his mother during one of his visits. "We needed money. She said, 'I'm going to go turn two or three tricks.' I told her, 'I'm going to try too, Mom.' I put on my leather jacket, I went where I had to go, and I did it with men. At first I was stressed. You don't know what might happen."

Despite a brief homosexual relationship, Jean-Loup considers himself heterosexual. He also believes that his imposing physique may be intimidating to certain clients. At twelve he had his first sexual experience with a girl of his age. His primary motive for hustling was money, and he says he realizes how big an effect his mother's example had on him: "She did it practically every day. At some point you feel like trying to make some money with it yourself. She always came home with money. I could see there was a lot to be made in this business." He made a brief incursion into escorting but disliked surrendering a share of his earnings, and he is now exclusively a street hustler. He quickly carved out a niche for himself.

"I have my street corner and nobody sits on my corner, even when I'm not there." His experience has been that hustlers close ranks in the face of the dangers represented by the police and bad tricks. "I know three-quarters of the guys on the street," he says. "We greet each other like buddies." For someone like himself with little schooling, he says, hustling is a practical trade requiring no special training: "If I wanted a job, I'd have to go back to school, and me and school, we don't get along. On my last day at school, I was so fed up that I threw my notebooks at the teacher's head." However, he thinks he would be good at computer science: "I've hacked into websites. A friend of mine who used to do that and got caught now works for the police. The thing is, I didn't get caught – maybe because I was better than him!"

Jean-Loup worked for some time as a messenger for a criminal gang, but after being shot at and having ribs broken, he gave it up without regrets: "It got way too dangerous." His experience appears to have convinced him that hustling is the only environment in which he really has his place. His vision of clients, though, is categorical: "A client is a walking wallet. They all think we're a bunch of drug addicts. But as for me, I don't take drugs really. I limit myself to alcohol, but my consumption is variable. I can be off it for days and then go on a binge."

By his own account, he spends his money wildly. His apartment is cheap, but he loves treating himself to computer hardware or a good restaurant meal. As a welfare recipient, he officially has only $275 per month to live on. Hustling, he says, provides the extra income he needs, and he sees no reason to quit. His physical strength gives him considerable self-assurance; he has no qualms about inviting clients (especially married men) home if they have nowhere else to suggest.

In terms of relationships, Jean-Loup was severely affected by the murder of his girlfriend last year. He was with a man for a while after that, but the relationship was dissatisfying and abortive: "His computer interested me more than he did ... And he never stopped telling everybody that he'd found me on the street. It was true, but why shout it from the rooftops? I care about my reputation. I'm not just a rag for you to wipe your ass on. I'm a human being who has to earn a living like everybody else."

He says he limits himself now to "fuck friends," young female acquaintances with whom he can have sex without commitment: "A fuck friend, you don't even give her breakfast. You fuck, she leaves, and that's it." Since he doesn't know these women well, he protects himself as much as with clients: "Because AIDS is part of my everyday life. I know quite a few people who have AIDS. I don't take risks." He is quite proactive in this respect, at least when he is on the wagon: "I always have mint-flavoured condoms on me. If I suck a guy off and there are secretions, or if his penis looks weird, I put the condom on. Anyway, I like the taste of mint in my mouth, not lubricant. It's simple: with a client, we do nothing without a condom, and he still owes me half the amount if we've already started. Besides which, I'm not big on blood tests, and that's why I don't take drugs: I hate needles! Most of the time the clients accept my conditions."

SID, A LIBERATIONIST

Sid has an air of the punk about him. He is the best educated of our respondents, having attended university, "just long enough to build up a whopping student loan debt of $21,000," he says bitterly. He went into sex work three years ago at age twenty-seven. His elderly parents live in a small, remote community; he maintains little contact with them so as to keep them unaware of his activities. He left home at seventeen after what he says was an ordinary childhood in an ordinary family, "civil servants who became the parents of two children in their forties and retired in their fifties, and now they wonder what to do with their lives." When he was about eighteen he had a girlfriend of the same age, but this was mainly out of a wish to conform. He broke off with her for lack of desire. He had sex for the first time at twenty-four, with an older man. "It took time before I started living out my fantasies, but I've sure caught up since then," he concludes.

Today, Sid has a boyfriend fifteen years his elder who lives in a distant Canadian city and whose health is precarious because he is HIV-positive. The lover has no problem with Sid's occupation and is not jealous. Sid has always been attracted by older men, a fact not unrelated to his profession and the pleasure it sometimes brings him. For Sid, physical appearance is not the most important part of attraction: dialogue, affinity, and emotional connection count for a great deal. These, he says, are the foundation of his love for a man he considers to be intellectually extraordinary.

Sid began to think about becoming a sex worker during a short prison term for petty larceny when a fellow prisoner offered him sex in return for protection. "I figured if I could do it under those conditions, not at all ideal, why wouldn't I try to do it elsewhere and earn an honest living?" He views the occupation from a rational perspective. He began as an escort and continues to practise independently through classifieds in newspapers and on the Internet (where we recruited him for this research). His clients are exclusively male because he does the job for pleasure and women do not attract him; he also declines requests from couples. He finds few sexual practices repulsive, though he prefers to project an active image and refuses any kind of domination or humiliation; apart from that, "It goes as far as the imagination can go, on one side or on the other." His clients range in age from eighteen to seventy-five, with a preponderance of older men. They are from all ethnic backgrounds: "I have slept with people from almost everywhere on the planet, all colours and religions." Generally, he does house calls or meets the client at a hotel, sauna, or similar location, spending as little as five minutes or as much as twelve hours: "It depends on the client's money and his level of excitement."

In terms of STD and AIDS prevention, Sid protects himself actively by stating his needs. Condoms are a must; he brings them in all sizes along with his own lubricant and massage oil. He uses latex gloves when he sees fit and avoids swallowing sperm. He takes drugs infrequently, drinks alcohol, and smokes hash, but not systematically or in such a way as to interfere with his self-control while working. With regular clients, he is open about his sexual tastes. "The more intimacy there is, the better, the more intense it'll be. In some cases it can almost become friendly. Especially with older men who learn to trust you, give you little gifts, take care of you ... It's important that I can be myself, do things I like, not change myself just to please people. The hardest part is to have active sex with someone who doesn't really attract me ... But whose fault is it if the guy's gross? Most clients are able to spot the difference between a hustler who does it for pleasure and one who only does it for money, drugs, or alcohol. That's why they appreciate me."

His personal needs being limited, Sid saves his money, acknowledging nonetheless that this is exceptional in his trade. Having done various odd jobs previously, he is convinced that sex work as he practises it is a good thing: "It's undoubtedly the most fun and creative way to earn my living, the one I have the most control over. Not to mention my self-confidence – my clients find my body more beautiful than I can imagine – and money that I couldn't have earned honestly in any other way. Freedom, also."

He does admit that one must be psychologically robust in order to cope with the hazards and consequences of the profession. When he feels depressed, he tells himself that it's not because of the job but because of how things went with a particular client or because business is slow. He deplores the stigma attached to what he does:

> It's just as respectable and honourable as any other job. Sharing two solitudes, the client's and the hustler's ... it's a human relationship. There are some really endearing people too, like this old, ugly, wrinkled guy who was just so sensitive ... He made me cry. I stayed with him the whole night, I just couldn't leave him, even though he only paid me for an hour! It's all the cameras focused on street prostitution, drug addicts, people who steal from clients, that's what gives us a bad image. When you charge an honourable price and get paid an honourable wage, you have no interest in losing your clients' trust ... And as for me, I actually like sex, I really like it. I like making love as much as possible every day. If I didn't I wouldn't be doing this job. I hope I'll be doing it for a long time. I want to stay young for a long time.

7

Contrasts and Resemblances

When we interview young sex workers, we are necessarily confronted with their visions of sex work and, in particular, their images of self and clients. The foregoing schematization of this material according to four basic life patterns points to significantly contrasting viewpoints – in fact, a few diametric oppositions – among these young men. These differences show that sex work responds to highly diverse interests and imperatives.

We paid particular attention to the ways in which these young men identify and perceive themselves, analyzing the visions they develop of their occupation and clientele. Figures 2, 3, and 4 below illustrate how the four life patterns correspond to differing or similar views on the following questions: Do sex workers identify with their work? Do they see their occupation as the result of a choice? Do they feel in control of their lives? How do they perceive their clients? Do they feel safe? What is their level of self-esteem?

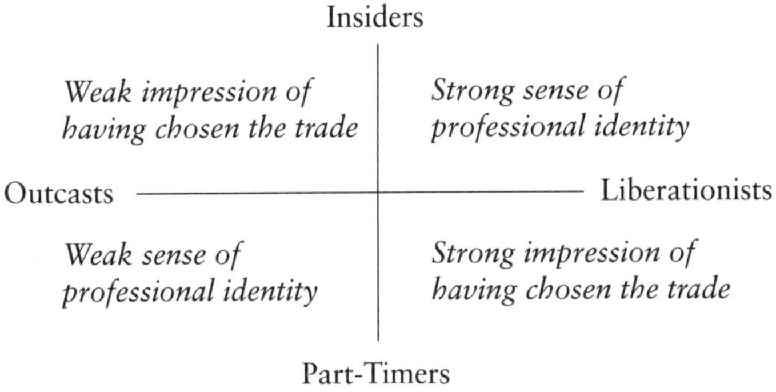

Insiders

| *Weak impression of having chosen the trade* | *Strong sense of professional identity* |

Outcasts ———————————————————— Liberationists

| *Weak sense of professional identity* | *Strong impression of having chosen the trade* |

Part-Timers

Figure 2

Figure 2 identifies two factors that stood out as clearly differentiating the respondents: whether or not they identify with the sex trade (regardless of the specific term they use to describe themselves) and whether or not they feel that their activities are the result of a conscious, rational choice, if only a temporary one.

This figure depicts how the answers to these two questions serve to elucidate the divides running through the four life patterns. The Outcasts perceive prostitution as a necessary evil if they are to procure drugs. It is not an activity they chose: it was and remains a matter of survival and dependency. For many it is no longer clear whether prostitution caused the addiction or vice versa. While some of these youths were not genuinely considering breaking their drug habit for good at the time of our interview, all deplored the fact that they had to hustle to feed it.

The Liberationists are the diametric opposite of the Outcasts along these axes; they evince a strong feeling of identification with their profession and generally assert it to be the result of a thoughtful choice. This is as one would expect from men who see prostitution as potentially gratifying and affirming. It cannot be overstressed that for them sex work is more than a way of making ready cash: it is a way of connecting with their own and their clients' inner lives and desires.

The Part-Timers, as we have noted, conceive of prostitution as a temporary activity resulting from a rational and enlightened choice, albeit one constrained by limited job opportunities. But as temporary workers by their own definition, they have little or no identification with the trade. They emphatically state that prostitution must remain circumstantial for them, that it must be partitioned off from the rest of their life (many are heterosexual and married, with children). Logically, then, they tend not to regard themselves as sex workers, much less prostitutes: they are in transition, earning money while waiting for other opportunities to arise.

By contrast, the Insiders' identification with the trade is strong indeed. As we have seen, prostitution is for them a family. Since they entered the profession in response to parental or peer influence, or other haphazard circumstances, they have little sense of having chosen the profession; quite the contrary, they give the impression of having been chosen by it.

In summary, the men we identified as Liberationists and Part-Timers consider their activities to be the result of a choice, while the Outcasts and Insiders tend to feel like

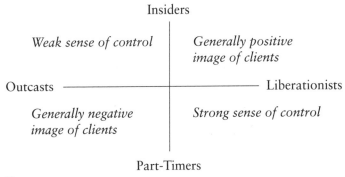

Figure 3

the victims of life's circumstances. On the question of self-identification, the lines of division are different. It is the Liberationists who have the strongest sense of identity as sex workers, followed closely by the Insiders, for whom the trade is in most cases their primary social circle. The Part-Timers and especially the Outcasts tend not to self-identify in this way; it is not and could not be their real profession, much less a driving force in their life. For these two groups, hustling appears more like an ad hoc solution to very different problems, whether it is the need for a fix or the need for greater material security.

As figure 3 indicates, the Part-Timers tend to feel that they have a degree of control over their working conditions. This is because they are able to keep their sex work cloistered so that it has no impact on their couple or family life. This sense of control is even stronger for the Liberationists, in whom it essentially becomes an act of will. The freedom and pleasure they seek would appear to necessitate a high level of self-control – not to mention control of the client, should he become demanding, unruly, or violent.

The reverse is true of the Outcasts, who seem to be willing to do just about anything when in urgent need of money, alcohol, or drugs. While these respondents initially claimed to observe prudence when confronting the risks of the trade, it became clear during our interview that their protective measures against STDs and AIDS – or lack of them – tend to be dictated by their immediate needs.

The Insiders' position on control was not as clear cut, but they often gave the impression of being in thrall to the trade and its rules and practices, hence less in control of themselves and their clients than they might hope. The heavy substance use by this group while on the job may further impair their faculties just when self-control is most needed.

As to their perceptions of their clients, figure 3 shows the Liberationists having the most positive outlook, followed closely by the Insiders, for whom clients are a part of their daily routine. Clients are not necessarily seen as friends, but neither are they enemies: they are just people who move within the same circles. The members of these two groups of sex workers have clients who become not only regulars but friends, protectors, or lovers and, therefore, positive influences on their lives, providing material or financial support, housing, advice, comfort, attention, intimacy, even affection.

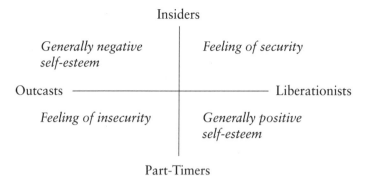

Figure 4

The Outcasts' view of clients stands in stark contrast: they see them as the persons responsible for their slavery as well as their moral, psychological, and/or physical decay. The Part-Timers are somewhere between these two poles; for them, the client is generally a means to an end, a way of making ends meet. The sooner they can move on, the better. Nevertheless, some Part-Timers admitted that they derived unexpected gratification from clients who were particularly caring, considerate, rich, or cultivated.

Figure 4 illustrates a third set of axes serving to differentiate the respondents, in this case by level of self-esteem and feeling of security or safety while on the job.

The Liberationists preserve a high level of self-esteem, perceiving their sex work as a social service offered to men who would otherwise be estranged or unhappy. As mentioned, most of these men like their jobs. They are conscious of societal prejudices against sex work but do not share them, and so remain unaffected by them. The Part-Timers too manage to maintain high self-esteem, but this is due to the mental and physical enclosures they keep around their paid sexual activity. They rationalize sex work as a springboard to advancement in life and as a means of overcoming temporary financial problems and other difficulties.

By contrast, the Insiders perceive themselves as at once the beneficiaries and the prisoners of their lifestyle. They have ups and downs, experiencing depression and suicidal ideation. For the Outcasts, with their double enslavement to drugs and prostitution and their sense of being society's "garbage can," the situation is even more sombre. Many have attempted suicide as a result of either or both of these problems, as well as a host of related ones.

On the question of security or safety, the Outcasts' drug dependency tends to produce strong feelings of insecurity. They are willing to risk having sex with unsavoury-looking clients or engaging in high-risk sexual practices, and they are keenly aware of the danger. For very different reasons, the Part-Timers also feel uneasy in the world of prostitution, a world that is never really their own. The heterosexual members of this group especially – and they are in the majority – find the complex codes of gay culture to be a constant source of uncertainty and uneasiness.

The opposite is true for the Liberationists, for whom sex work is pre-eminently a comfortable life choice, at least for a certain period of time. They feel at ease in their job and the environment surrounding it. Finally, the Insiders see themselves as being rather like children of the circus when it comes to prostitution: they feel relatively comfortable in this circle, despite the problems, tensions, and conflicts that inevitably arise. They have the impression of having learned to "land on their feet," of being able to confront the hazards of the trade with a degree of assurance.

Summarizing this discussion, we have identified six factors (identification with sex work, feeling of control, rational choice of sex work, image of clients, self-esteem, and feeling of security or safety) illustrating the differences, even oppositions, among sex workers who exhibit the four life patterns. It is as if divergent viewpoints, contrary states of mind – indeed, radically different existential philosophies – coexist, overlap, and telescope within the same world.

A last remark is in order regarding the question – so central to debates over female prostitution – of power relations between clients and sex workers. If our respondents' accounts are to be believed, one gets the impression that with the Liberationists at least, if not necessarily with the other groups, power actually resides more with the prostitute than with his clients. If he is free of drug addiction, if he can set rates and schedules and select clients, the prostitute clearly has a degree of power and control over his working conditions. If, in addition, he has the ability to set his terms regarding STD and HIV risks (we examine this issue in the next chapter), it is difficult to conclude that all male sex workers are slaves to their environment, their clients, or the sex entrepreneurs. This does not mean that male prostitution is an ideal job, nor even a job "like any other," but merely that it comprises a highly diverse range of living conditions. It is a multifarious phenomenon that corresponds, as we have seen, to different life scenarios and personal needs.

8

Risks of the Trade

Even those young men who see obvious advantages in sex work admit that it entails multiple dangers and pitfalls. For street hustlers especially, violence looms at every turn. One recounted an incident in which a client stole the little money he had. Another told of being raped and beaten by a group of young drunks in an apparently homophobic crime, then abandoned, naked, far outside the city on a deserted road. In addition to these hazards, there may be continual skirmishes among sex workers for control of a street corner, or altercations with clients and drug dealers. Many sex entrepreneurs such as bar or agency managers regard independent operators as a threat and may respond in kind, yet as employers they can and do fire employees without notice as well as unilaterally determining their working conditions. The police and other moral entrepreneurs are, of course, always to be shunned. In short, prostitution is an unpredictable, high-risk activity, even for the most physically or psychologically robust of young men. All the while, hanging over their heads like a sword of Damocles is the threat of losing their place in the fragile hierarchy of prostitution, with younger, better-looking, more popular men always ready to take over and many clients eager to give them a whirl.

Whereas strippers and escorts appear somewhat better protected against physical violence, they can never be certain how things will turn out once they find themselves alone with a client. After all, though much noise is made about substance abuse among sex workers (especially Outcasts), their clients are quite conversant with the same substances, making for a potentially explosive cocktail. Almost all our respondents have been marked by experiences in which clients assaulted them, threatened them with a weapon, underwent a mental or physical breakdown in their presence, or aggressively refused to pay the bill. In most cases there is no question of reporting such incidents to the police, who are perceived as nothing but a source of additional problems. Besides, as one respondent asked rhetorically, whose story will be believed, that of the prostitute or the "upstanding citizen"?

Regarding the risks of HIV and STD transmission, the impression left by the respondents is by turns reassuring and worrisome. While many sex workers apparently insist on protecting themselves adequately, others – the Outcasts, notably – may be willing to do anything to support their drug habit. Intravenous drug users are doubly at risk, through both sex and injections. Certain Insiders, too, let down their guard and take more risks when under the influence of alcohol or drugs, a typical feature of their lifestyle. The diseases contracted by our study group include HIV (five respondents), hepatitis, condylomas, scabies, and crab lice.

The Part-Timers, meanwhile, are systematically prudent in protecting themselves against STDs and AIDS, for they do not wish the impacts of their "occasional" sex work to carry over into their private, couple, or family life. (Most are married with children.) Finally, the Liberationists appear to be at greater risk in their private lives than their professional lives; moreover, the two may overlap at times in such a way as to impair their self-protective reflexes. A few respondents from all groups made clear that money is certainly not their only concern: "You're not going to risk your life for an extra twenty bucks!"

As Maurice Tubiana relevantly observes in *L'Éducation et la vie*, to take a risk is to accept a hazard in order to derive a benefit. Risk and hazard are not synonyms, since a hazard is an objective threat while a risk implies simultaneous consideration of hazard and gain.[19] For our purposes, the risk in question involves accepting the hazard of contracting STDs or HIV in order to have a physically, mentally, or materially gratifying sexual relationship. One can, of course, attempt to minimize the likelihood of occurrence of a hazard and hence the risk associated with the corresponding benefit. This is precisely the kind of calculus that many sex workers perform when contemplating various kinds of physical contact with their clients.

Tubiana delineates three types of risk:

1 *Objective* risk is statistically calculable risk, the actual likelihood of occurrence of the hazard. The level of risk for our purposes depends, of course, on the sex act performed and the persons involved; specifically, it depends on the degree of certainty that any of them carries a transmissible disease as well as the objective probability of transmission as a result of the act. Simply put, having certain kinds of sex with certain people entails a higher objective risk than others.

2 *Perceived* risk is necessarily subjective and may be underestimated out of habit, indifference, or a false sense of security. As we shall see below, this is in fact the case for numerous sex workers vis-à-vis their regular clients.

3 *Accepted* risk is that which is perceived as being natural, inevitable, or even desirable. This type of attitude was mainly observed among the drug-addicted street hustlers in our survey.

The German author Michael Bochow stresses that most people's existential logic is of a different species from the public health logic of STD and HIV prevention. Negative explanations of risk-taking – lack of information, control, skills, means, and so on – cannot be neglected, but neither do they fully answer the inevitable question, "Why do people take risks when they have sex?" Bochow therefore sets this question aside in favour of the simpler, "Why do people have sex?"[20] In regard to sex workers, an answer to this second question helps us answer the first, which is of course a central concern of our study. This requires that we enlarge our focus to all the positive factors (emotional, love related, erotic, fantasy related, material, situational) that influence behaviour itself, sexual behaviour included. Too often risk-taking is regarded in a negative light or as a lack of information, control, or ability. The reality is more complex.

In the strategies they use with their clients, sex workers are exemplars of this calculus: each tries to maximize his gratification (sex, money, drugs, affection, etc.) while minimizing the hazards inherent in his sexual practices. From this standpoint, protecting oneself against STDs or HIV is less a matter of believing that all hazards can be eliminated than of confronting them with one's available strengths and resources.

Our respondents' comments indicate that most of them grasp the objective risks surrounding STDs and AIDS. The messages of prevention have generally come across loud and clear. However, the perceived risks are, for many, a different story. They feel that they have little power to control them, particularly when their need for money or drugs is pressing. Hence, for these individuals, perceived and accepted risks coincide. For this reason the Outcasts and the Insiders appear to be at greater risk of STD and HIV transmission than the Part-Timers, the most self-protective group, so as to avoid bringing home the undesirable outcomes of their work, and the Liberationists, in whom a clear desire for control is always perceptible. After all, the latter two groups adopted prostitution as a conscious choice, so it is only natural that their health – an essential component of personal satisfaction and quality of life – be a constant concern for them.

Consequently, it is no surprise to find Part-Timers – the group most concerned about AIDS and STDS – expressing distaste for sperm and even saliva as possible disease vectors: "To avoid kissing or sucking the client, I give the excuse that I've just brushed my teeth or that I have fragile gums. My message is that certain activities can be dangerous, as much for him as for me. It puts a damper on certain impulses."

But it is not easy for prostitutes to insist on the wearing of a condom, as it could intimate to the client that he looks sick or arouses distrust: "You have to go easy, diplomatically, without upsetting him. It's not good to disappoint the client." Several respondents expressed the seemingly paradoxical idea that their "passivity" during sex could offer some protection. One heterosexual man commented: "The client is the one doing something for me, if you see what I mean. And if he gives a good blow-job, well, a mouth is a mouth ... If he manages to really excite me, which is pretty rare, I'll give him one too, but I never, ever, ever swallow cum. As for anal, forget it!"

Obviously, clients are not always convinced by such excuses. Several respondents admitted that clients can be lost for good if they sense that their wishes (oral-genital or anal relations, for example) are being deliberately foiled. When they pay for sex, clients expect to be allowed to live out all their fantasies; the last thing they want is to inspire distrust or reticence on the part of the person who is supposed to provide sexual pleasure and excitement.

Whereas the majority of the Part-Timers claim that their heterosexuality "naturally" protects them from HIV transmission because of their reserves or repulsion towards homosexual practices, their relations with female clients avowedly take place without apprehension or protection. This reflects a widespread truth among all the respondents, irrespective of sexual orientation and life pattern, that mutual desire, trust, or intimacy between sex worker and client can cause prevention to go by the wayside. "I trusted her, she seemed honest, so I let it happen without a condom," said one man. "Sometimes I don't see any need to protect myself," admitted another. "I don't get the impression that it could be dangerous. These are people that I've known for some time, they don't seem to have any health or disease problems or whatever."

Intimacy, confidence, and friendship do not easily coexist with fear or wariness, another fact noted by Bochow. While the foreign is forbidding, the familiar can be reassuring. Thus, the regularity of a relationship, albeit professional, can lead the sex worker to abandon his usual preventive measures. On this point one young man concluded, "There is no man who will protect himself all the time. It's not easy, and besides, it depends on the relationship, the partner. I'm a responsible man,

I don't want to give anybody diseases, but I protect myself in maybe 80 per cent of my relationships."

Among Part-Timers and Insiders particularly, frequent HIV testing (at three- to six-month intervals) and careful observation of the client's body are routine. These practices are a way of exorcising danger and, so may offer a false sense of security. One sex worker with mainly female clients stated: "I've had some clients for five, six, seven years. They get tested every three months like I do. I show a client my test results, she shows me hers, and we can skip the protection. That's my protection, that medical note." Another, with a large majority of male clients, stated: "I carefully examine the client's genitals. If the head of his penis has sores, if he has condylomas, if there's anything out of the ordinary, I follow my intuition."

Such statements recall the concept of imaginary protection developed by Rommel Mendès-Leite. He explains that individuals tend to reinterpret and adapt the social rules of prevention to the circumstances, all the while continuing to believe that their level of risk is minimal.[21] The tactics of imaginary protection include selecting partners by appearance, sex, sexual orientation, or socioeconomic status ("when he takes you to a really nice house, you're more inclined to trust him"); letting friendship interfere with safer sex practices; getting AIDS tested as a form of exorcism, and possessing a condom totemically without actually using it. We observed all these tactics among our respondents.

The Insiders are undoubtedly the group with the largest number of HIV-infected friends, and so their fear is the most palpable: "When they started dropping like flies around us, whether it was friends, friends of friends, that's when I woke up! Especially since most of the clients, it's like they don't think about that. The married men, especially, they think that because they're only sleeping with a guy one time, it won't happen to them. So I have to tell them, "Listen, these days, all the diseases going around ... I'm not saying that I have it [AIDS] or that you have it, but we won't take any risks, we don't know each other. Sorry, but it's condom or nothing."

More fatalistically, another concluded, "In this business there's always danger. A condom can break, you know. You're talking to a professional, OK? It doesn't matter where I am or with whom, there's always danger, always a risk. You have to accept it."

The Insiders tend to adopt a double standard with regard to regular versus occasional clients, as one respondent explained: "Occasional clients can get the little job [mutual masturbation or a blow-job quickly given or received]. The big job, full intercourse, anal sex – that's for regulars." The double standard can be partially explained by the intimacy that develops between sex workers and regular clients, which some of our respondents compared to a filial or couple relationship. After all, a friend is someone who normally inspires trust, and especially so if he appears to bear us good will. The scarcity of this in the world of sex work may make it all the more desirable, thus heightening the workers' psychological and physical vulnerability to friendlier or more familiar clients. On this subject, one respondent said, "The regular client is somebody that you have to keep. There's more intimacy with him, and more respect also. You won't tell him that you brushed your teeth to avoid having to suck him off. You can kiss him, take your shower with him, like real lovers. You'll also have to reciprocate and give him a blow-job."

The Liberationists, as we have seen, perceive their work as a kind of playtime activity, at least at the outset. It is a way of living out their desires and fantasies. Their relationship to sex work is quite different from that of their colleagues, and the different point of view affects their perception of risk. The Liberationists protect themselves primarily because, as sex workers who consciously strive to satisfy their emotional and sexual needs on the job, they take their health concerns to heart:

I have minimum standards that I must always respect.

The danger is not in blow-jobs, not even in penetration, which people see as the biggest risk. The dangerous thing is to lose control. If the client is really determined, I might do it without a condom, but I'm the one in control.

Occasional clients, I'm not afraid to control them. I'm going to control them. If an occasional client becomes regular, it's because I've learned to control him, calm him down, and he liked it. I always stay in control.

The problem is the people, whether it's clients or hustlers, who lose their head when they're too stoned or drunk. You always have to stay in control, regardless of what stage you're at. That's the most important thing.

But when strong desire comes into play, the client is no longer so willing to be controlled, as one respondent concedes. "I can't stand cum, I avoid it, I've never swallowed any in my life … Except once it did happen, yes, that I gave a complete blow-job to a young client who I was really attracted to. He really drove me wild."

Despite their vigilance, some Liberationists and others may become more vulnerable to STD and HIV transmission when they become friends or lovers with clients and let down their guard. In this sense, enjoyment of sex may serve as a soporific, closing their eyes to the dangers inherent in the act. But the sudden awareness that pleasure has vanished because of the client's demands may have the reverse effect of waking them up to their loss of control, which Liberationists regard as the real danger.

With the Outcasts, there is often a great divide between the way they operate in practice and the principles they claim to have assimilated. Undoubtedly most have heard the messages of STD and AIDS prevention, but a pressing need for money or drugs may get the better of their initial intent to protect themselves. "I didn't want anything to do with clients who wanted it without a condom, but for a large sum of money I did it. It

didn't happen often, but I did do it," one admitted.
Similarly, another told us, "If the client doesn't want to
put on a condom, he can go somewhere else ... although when I really needed money and the client offered the right price ..."

For most, fellatio represents a calculated risk, "as long
as there's no ejaculation in the mouth." But for drug-
addicted Outcasts, needle sharing remains the highest-
risk behaviour with respect to HIV transmission:

> My risky behaviour is shooting up. There are times
> when I'm so fucked up I don't know whose needles
> are whose.

> Needle-sharing was my biggest risk.

> I got AIDS from the needles I used to pick up anywhere.

Due to the direr circumstances under which they live
and work, the Outcasts are less willing to risk losing a
client due to insistence on safer sex than are the members of the other three groups: "I would never ask a client to put on a condom if I was sure it would make him
change his mind and fuck off." Some of these young
men regret having driven clients away by insisting on
prevention too pointedly: "Most of the clients totally
hate putting on a condom. I've lost a few just because
of that. One night, for once I'd picked up a really good-
looking young guy and everything, I was so pissed off
when I lost him."

A number of respondents admitted that their insistence on safer sex falls by the wayside when their mental state is altered by alcohol or drugs: "When I'm stoned or drunk, I lose my head. When I do it without a condom, it's always because of alcohol or damn drugs." Worse still, some come to consider themselves invulnerable when their repeated risk-taking fails to produce any ill effects. They may even see their failure to use protection as a kind of extreme sport or "ordalic behaviour" in the sense of Le Breton[22] – that is, the taking of a potentially fatal risk in a quasi-ritual manner, leaving the final judgment to the will of God. The following comments by three respondents are eloquent on this point:

> I've never really protected myself too much and I never got anything. I thank my lucky stars for that. I've always turned out to be HIV-negative. The other day I shot up with somebody's needles, I don't know whose, and I slept with a girl I met in a shooting gallery, without any protection. I know I have hepatitis C. Sometimes I put on a condom and sometimes not. When I was younger, I picked up needles in the street. I let myself be penetrated without a condom. I absolutely couldn't care less about HIV. I don't understand. I have some friends who did a foolish thing once and got AIDS. I'm going to get tested again. But I'm like those prostitutes in an African country who don't develop AIDS. They do all kinds of things and they don't catch the disease. I think of myself as invincible. I tell myself it won't happen to me.

If I do a line of coke before fucking, I'm not so afraid of the risks. I need to do that pretty often with the clients and the guys I hang out with. Yes, I'm playing with fire. Every day I tell myself that maybe today I'm going to get AIDS, or maybe I'll survive again ... You might say I'm toying with it. It's like I'm tossing the dice. If my number comes up, AIDS, too bad for me; if not, well, all right, then!

As for me, I don't give a shit about AIDS. If I have it, I couldn't care less. Sometimes I think I must be running after it, because there's nothing I haven't done ... I always used to consider myself infected. I told myself I had AIDS, that there was no point protecting myself anymore or wanting to live. I wasn't protecting myself.

Their traumatic experiences in childhood and subsequently may cause Outcasts to feel degraded in ways that affect their self-esteem and even their desire to live. Some seem to be consciously bent on self-destruction: "Prostitution fucks with your life and your sexuality. At first you close your eyes, but at some point you realize what you're doing and your self-esteem takes a big hit. Me, I wanted to die, to kill myself. After years of hustling you're not a human being anymore, and you get fed up with sex. With everything, in fact."

Those of our respondents who are HIV-positive only rarely inform their clients of that fact:

I had no consciousness of what I was doing. I was only doing it so I could get stoned. All I saw was a body and, behind it, a needle. That was all I saw, nothing else. I was somewhere else, I wasn't myself anymore.

For money, or to make a client happy, I'll have unsafe sex, even though there's a chance I have AIDS. After all, my lover has AIDS.

You're like the garbage can of society, you have a hard time asserting yourself, saying no to what they ask you [unprotected sex], that's how bad you need a fix. If I had a needle in my arm, I would share it with anybody. I had unprotected anal relations. I was playing with my life. I didn't love myself.

For some of the Outcasts, HIV testing offers a kind of symbolic, *post hoc* protection when panic strikes. We also observed that intravenous drug-using prostitutes were, on average, less assiduous condom users with female partners than those of their colleagues whose clientele is exclusively male.[23] As to relations with their life partner, these are generally unprotected unless one of them is known to be HIV-positive. It is as if awareness of HIV transmission risks evaporates outside the context of prostitution, and especially in the presence of true intimacy, even when the partner is also a sex worker.

Like their colleagues, the Outcasts are more inclined to trust regular or attractive clients, to feel safe with them and eventually relate to them as friends or confidants (something rare in their lives), but this means that they are more willing to allow anal relations and less likely to use safer sex practices: "The regular clients, yeah, we'll do them," said one interviewee. "We spend time together, we spend the night, we chat, sometimes we have oral sex, masturbation, blow-jobs." Explained another, "There are times where I sincerely believe there's no danger because I know the person. I've known them for so long! I know there's no danger." Regular clients are often the only adults whom sex workers, especially street hustlers, can trust or ask for help. Outcasts are so devoid of bearings and starved for affection that regulars can rapidly turn into father or big brother figures. Such a kindly person could not do me harm, they assume, yet the harm in question – STD or HIV transmission, among other possibilities – is a very dire prospect.

It cannot be emphasized too strongly that the sex worker's mental state greatly influences his ability to engage in the negotiation that is a feature of every commercial transaction. When the sex worker hands a condom to a client or other partner, the implicit message of caring for both parties' well-being may be interpreted as an intimation that the client represents a threat. As sex workers well know, it may be seen as an unfriendly, anti-erotic gesture. The situation becomes even more complicated if the youth's diminished self-worth leads him to believe he does not really deserve protection.

Young male sex workers, regardless of category, are members of various socially marginalized and vulnerable groups. They are young, they have sex with men, and they have multiple partners; many of them are substance abusers and sexual-abuse survivors; some have had problems with the law. These latter factors, especially, go some distance in explaining why they so often perceive themselves as lacking any real power over their lives. And while their knowledge of AIDS transmission risks is thorough enough, it does not always deter them from engaging in unsafe sex, especially with non-clients and regulars or where their sex work is driven by drug addiction. Furthermore, in an environment in which appearance trumps reality, magical thinking, contradictions, half-truths, and lies are common currency. This is the price to be paid for the momentary illusion of shared seduction and pleasure.

9

When They Need Help

Though some boys seem inevitably bound for prostitution, there is nothing predestined about this outcome. Conversely, while some sex workers appear to have chosen their profession, their choice was generally conditioned by a limited array of possibilities. For all our respondents without exception, sex work was or remains a solution to one or more problems: drug addiction, indebtedness or other financial problems, the need to experience a different lifestyle, the search for a social circle, or the search for recognition or affection (this last being typical of those who have experienced parental rejection). In this respect it was a relative choice, a choice that responded to certain problems or needs. What we are saying is that before prostitution becomes a problem for society – by the actions of the moral entrepreneurs especially – and for its practitioners (and their clients), it is perceived by these young men as a solution, or at any rate a lesser evil.

And so, if sex workers rarely ask for help, it may be because they feel that they have already found their solution. It is only when the gap between expectation and reality becomes too wide that they begin to question their involvement in sex work. That is the moment when they are most open to seeking or accepting certain forms of assistance such as employment and other counselling, back-to-school assistance, health services, and suitable housing.

But until he has reached a critical threshold of dissatisfaction, no sex worker will consider giving up his work, for he sees no reason why he should. He will be particularly unreceptive to offers of help from outside his milieu. Professionals in general have a rather bad reputation with him, and not without reason. Police are perceived as natural enemies whose sole aim is to catch sex workers in the act. Social workers (with whom some of these youths have had dealings since childhood) are ineffectual and sermonizing. Health services are not always sensitive to their concerns or adapted to their lifestyle and pace; for example, they may not offer late hours.

Yet there is nothing inscrutable about sex workers' needs. They need to be free of judgment and stigma. They want to be respected by clients, neighbours, and fellow citizens as full-fledged members of society, possessing the same rights and responsibilities. They want access to the same quality of health care and legal services. At times they are looking for a sympathetic ear that can hear their anguish or listen to their self-doubt. But the fear of prejudice at best and repression at worst often deters them from seeking such services, whose purveyors are generally perceived as closed-minded if not openly hostile to their activities, and hence to themselves. In most cities there are few or no public or quasi-public services directed specifically at young male sex workers. Society simply closes its eyes to their existence.

Our respondents told us that they never considered reporting to the police any violence they experienced at the hands of clients or colleagues, convinced that doing so would only compound their problems. While recent years have witnessed an improvement in relations between sex workers and helping professionals including street workers and community nurses, much remains to be done in terms of resource availability. For example, a young man applying for drug rehabilitation may be unwilling to talk openly about his sex work, central to his life though it may be. Regardless of his sexual orientation (for it is a widespread misconception in society that all male sex workers are gay), he may fear becoming the object of homophobic prejudice.

Another hurdle for sex workers to overcome is the search for a new job, if they should decide to look for one. No employer acknowledges their experience as having any value; on the contrary, most perceive it as something negative, degrading and contemptible. Where the job market is concerned, these men are usually better off keeping their past a secret. A return to school, through adult education or other programs, can be equally challenging. It is another world, a different pace and lifestyle. The transition is difficult. Thus, most of our respondents, even those who had ceased their sex-work activities, remained in or on the periphery of prostitution. They were lucky to find work in a gay bar or, for those who did some bodybuilding, at the gym where they trained. Some young gays or bisexuals find an alternative in the form of a "sugar daddy" with whom they can lead a relatively comfortable couple life – but for how long?

Sex work, then, offers no easy exit. This is true even for men who are not under the thumb of pimps as such, for drug dealers can keep them subjugated equally well. The debts that many of our respondents accrue as a result of their drug habit are direct incentives to remain in the trade beyond the point when they know it is time to quit. Thus, breaking the drug habit becomes a corequisite for getting out of prostitution. These comments, of course, apply particularly to the Outcasts and the Insiders.

In sum, what these young men need is a variety of resources that are better adapted to their needs. Housing must be provided for the most destitute, those youths who survive from one client to the next, seeking no more than food and a place to sleep. In terms of health services, the existing small-scale, quasi-personal initiatives to offer preventive and curative services on the sites of sex work are insufficient and should be expanded. Detoxification centres treating sex workers must reassure them that they will not be labelled or marginalized. Sympathetic legal and police services must genuinely help them face the problems they encounter in prostitution (indebtedness, violence, etc.) rather than ignoring them or, worse, persecuting these men for their problems, or threatening such persecution. Finally, there is a need for employment counsellors and programs that give due consideration to the life experience of these young men when they begin to look for other work.

Our survey indicates that, by and large, young sex workers are dealing with the same issues as many other people their age: personal growth challenges, career options, love and sex, drug and alcohol addiction, strained familial relations, and so forth. However, their resources are more limited, and so is their inclination to seek outside help. Practising a profession disparaged by much of the population, fearing a re-enactment of earlier rejections, most young sex workers keep their activities and problems from friends and relations, trusting almost no one. Those with the greatest need for assistance are the ones most left to their own devices.

Yet several of our respondents' histories betray evident needs arising from their past. The scars of sexual abuse may be reopened with each new non-reciprocal encounter with a client; chronic low self-esteem may keep these youth isolated or lead to suicidal ideation; parental or familial rejection may still be painful years after the event. And their past on the margins often puts more conventional work options beyond their reach.

Consequently, considerable encouragement and accompaniment is necessary for them to even contemplate a break with prostitution, as dissatisfying as they may find it. One must admit that these young men have shown uncommon ingenuity and courage in overcoming the hurdles of their profession, but these same feats have left many of them fatigued and alone as they face their future.

Our society does not promise marginal people a positive destiny, and young sex workers, as we have indicated, are marginal in many respects. As children, many did not receive benevolent parental attention or adult understanding when they needed it, and some were abandoned outright by their parents. As young homosexuals or bisexuals in particular, they may have experienced painful rejection; one boy was caught in the act at age eleven and kicked out of the house. Many of them have had no real contact with their families of origin since childhood or adolescence. And, as has been shown, these problems are compounded by substance addiction, legal problems, and more. When these boys were in crisis, no one was there to listen or understand.

Disinterested sermon-free support is all too rare. Moreover, when services such as street workers and support groups are available, they are often underused. As much as these youths yearn for authentic and sincere human contact, they have been taught to distrust, and so their trust must be earned. Even within the world of sex work itself, competition generally prevails over mutual aid. Therefore, the helping professionals who work with this population must be given the training, information, and specialization necessary to respond to its needs.

To acknowledge the existence of male sex work is not to encourage or discourage it but, rather, and quite simply, to state a fact. We may be moved or troubled by it, but it happens to be the product of a culture that idealizes the association between youth and sex even as its taboos confine certain sexualities to clandestinity. Young male prostitution is in some sense the mirror of the society from which it emerges, but for its practitioners it can be a burdensome existence. At the very least we could do them the service of lending an attentive ear to their concerns.

Afterword

The interest awakened by this research project upon its initial publication in French far outstripped all expectations, including the publisher's. Manifestly, the little-known world of male sex work arouses the public's curiosity as much as that of the media. The large number of subsequent public debates and interviews in which I participated enabled me to develop or clarify certain aspects of the subject. This afterword is an opportunity for me to respond to the most frequent questions I was asked about male sex work and to conclude on a somewhat more personal note.

The first obvious conclusion arising from our study is that male sex work is not a unitary phenomenon but, rather, a multifaceted one. The motivations, rationales, and life patterns of our respondents varied to such an extent that we opted to divide them into four distinct groups. Between the Outcast who hustles to feed his drug habit and the Liberationist who dances or prostitutes himself for the feeling of personal pleasure it brings, there is indeed a world of difference. Likewise, the difference is great between the Part-Timer attempting to supplement his income without the knowledge of friends or family and the Insider for whom the world of prostitution in fact represents his "family," his only social circle. Furthermore, a whole continuum of intermediate patterns stretches between these groups. There is not one but several forms of sex work and even more ways to enter, contemplate, or practise this profession – perhaps almost as many as there are sex workers. Thus both the view of sex work as a plague on society and the view in which it is a profession much like any other find support and challenge in our study. After all, we did our best to gather the full range of sex workers' views, giving as much attention to those who feel victimized by their environment as to those who feel in control of it. These differences were due, as we saw, to the type of sex work practised, the conditions under which it occurs, the problems encountered, and the sex worker's image of himself, his activities, and his clients.

The most underexplored aspect in the body of research on prostitution concerns the relationships between clients and sex workers, especially those that are not exclusively sexual in nature. Our knowledge of clients is most often derived from sex workers' perceptions – not without interest (far from it), but biased nonetheless.[24] This is as may be expected, as most clients carefully preserve their anonymity; yet to my surprise several of them wrote to me after reading the French version of this book. It was interesting to note that their accounts are entirely consistent with those of the sex workers we interviewed. Some defined themselves as curious heterosexuals or as bisexuals leading a double life. They greatly feared being identified and having their activities revealed to friends, relatives, or acquaintances. Even those who acknowledged their homosexuality tended to keep their use of sexual services a secret. Some said they do not want to be perceived as being unable to find other partners due to their age or physical characteristics that exclude them from the "gay seduction market." Others mentioned that paying for sex allows them to control the situation or have the impression of doing so.

A relationship between a client and a sex worker differs from others in that it is the client alone who decides on its length and the limits of his emotional or physical involvement. Some men view their use of sexual services as a way of exploring an aspect of their sexuality privately and under controlled conditions. Although a degree of friendship or complicity may develop over time, the reciprocity and commitment characteristic of friendships and love relationships are generally absent.

Nevertheless, the exchange taking place in prostitution is not merely that of consensual sex for money. It is also a symbolic exchange which, for the client especially, entails a *mise en scène* of fantasy elements such as beauty, power, money, youth, and seduction. Without these the sexual attraction or excitement provoked by the sex worker would probably not occur. Clients' fantasies and erotic scenarios, the sociosexual roles they act out or demand, are among the least known yet most decisive aspects of the demand for male (not to mention female) prostitution. Inventive research strategies that can tell us more about clients and their experiences would be welcome.

Another question often asked concerns the existence or absence of male prostitution rings. According to the accounts we gathered, small, ultra-clandestine operations do exist but mainly involve underage boys. They are maintained by men with strong pedophilic tendencies who essentially recruit and exchange children or adolescents for purposes of sex or pornography (which has, of course, undergone an unprecedented explosion on the Internet). Because of the men's sexual preferences, these rings do not involve adult prostitutes; after the age of fourteen to sixteen, a boy is no longer considered attractive to them. If he continues in sex work beyond that age – often to pay for a drug habit acquired while under the influence of his "protectors" – he will largely do so as a freelancer.[25] It is not surprising that so many of these boys eventually find themselves hustling on the street, only a few managing to become strippers and escorts.

This is very different from the situation of girl prostitution, most of which takes place within large rings under the control of pimps and organized crime. Girls may have ten or more clients per day for periods of many years, yielding major profits. They are valuable to prostitution rings well beyond the age of majority and are not easily let go.

Should escort agencies be considered prostitution rings? I tend to think not. Agencies generally employ adults only. Their main purpose is to serve as intermediary between two consenting adults, a client and a sex worker, monitor the engagement, and provide some protection against violent clients. For these services they take a percentage of the profits. There is little of the quasi-slavery involving threats, blackmail, or carefully cultivated emotional or drug dependency that characterizes prostitution rings. Such organizations are interested in controlling people, not employing them, and they pay little or nothing to the children and young adults under their domination. Any "protection" they may offer usually favours the clients, who are allowed or even encouraged to commit violent or sadistic acts. No agency would tolerate such things; if it did, few people would be willing to work for it. I am by no means likening escort agencies to works of charity; I am saying that they are far less dangerous and criminalized than prostitution rings. Clearly, these rings are of little or no interest to adult male sex workers and vice versa. None of the respondents in our study, for example, was involved in a ring or had a pimp (a role generally linked to organized crime) at the time of our interview.

Another difference between agencies and prostitution rings is the latter's extensive use of hard drugs as a means of keeping young people under their control, for, as is well known, inducing a psychotropic addiction in vulnerable people is one of the surest ways to render them dependent. Agencies tend to discourage drug use because they want to ensure that clients get their money's worth, that is, someone in full possession of his faculties. Obviously, this does not mean that escorts never take drugs in private or at a client's behest, but a serious substance abuser is unlikely to remain for long on an agency list.

Are new phenomena emerging in male sex work? They are, and this reflects greater diversity in the demand for sexual services. While male prostitution was formerly synonymous with youth (unlike female prostitution, which has always covered a broader age range), an increasing number of men in their thirties and even forties are now doing this work. The reason is that the clients themselves are more diverse. Some of our respondents noted, for example, that female and couple clients, who create a demand for more mature men, appear to be growing in numbers. As well, emerging sex work opportunities (erotic phone-line workers, home striptease artists, erotic masseurs, and porno film actors, for example) targeting both male and female clients make it possible for many men to earn a living in this field where once they would not have dreamed of doing so. The rent boy need not even be particularly attractive: in the vast market aimed at exploiting unquenched fantasies, there is something for every taste – and it is advertised with increasing openness.

Sex work and prostitution will remain controversial themes for much time to come. Although used synonymously in this work, the two terms also signify a recurring ideological opposition in the literature and the public mind. Where some argue that the term "sex worker" trivializes a serious problem, others are equally adamant that the term "prostitute" should be avoided because of the load of negative connotations it carries. All of us are prone to the temptations of moral entrepreneurship – deciding what is intrinsically good or bad for society – but be that as it may, there is no reason to avoid learning about the world of prostitution from the point of view of its practitioners. Not only can their fellow citizens learn much from their experiences but allowing them to speak is a way of acknowledging their humanity and intelligence, which are too often denied.

As to what may be the desirable legal status of prostitution, I can honestly state that I had hardly any preconceived ideas on this point at the outset. However, this study and subsequent experiences have led me to take a position. Insofar as I believe that sex workers should be protected from abuse by clients, rings, pimps, agencies, and the moral entrepreneurs who pursue them, that they should enjoy the same rights and freedoms as any other citizen, and that the state should not intervene in private sexual relations between fully consenting adults, I would tend to favour the option of decriminalization, as do most organizations advocating on behalf of sex workers. Society has enough problems helping people young or old who are intimidated, threatened, or abused, whether they are working as

prostitutes or in other walks of life, without the added
complications caused by making their work illegal. I
hasten to reiterate my awareness that sex work is not
always chosen and that it does not always takes place
under ideal conditions – all the more reason, then, for
society to intervene where youths are held prisoner by
gangs, mistreated by clients, harassed by drug dealers,
or otherwise in need of our help. No one should be
forced to prostitute himself, whether for economic,
emotional, or other reasons; everything possible should
be done to give him other alternatives. But none of this
requires banning prostitution outright. Our legal frame-
work is sufficient to protect any person, including a sex
worker, who is victimized by another – provided, of
course, that the laws are enforced. We also, as a society,
have the resources necessary to help prostitutes move
on in life, as long as these are made genuinely available,
accessible, and welcoming.

Nevertheless, those who tell us that they do sex work
by choice (within the limited range of choices available
to each of us, naturally) must be heard. I am the first to
admit that I would like to live in a world where such
work has no reason for being, where all of us could fulfil
our desires for affection, eroticism, and sexuality readily
and naturally while helping our partners do the same.
We are far from living in such an Eden. A necessary step
towards bringing it about is to develop a more caring,
tolerant society, a society that reaches out to marginalized individuals such as the young people who practise

sex work. To treat them as either criminals or perpetual victims (in either case, presumably, without critical consciousness or free will) only further marginalizes and infantilizes them, if it does not ostracize them altogether.

My small research team and I make no claim to having exhausted the subject of male prostitution. This study was a first and, at times, arduous step along the way. Our portrait of sex work might have been more complete if we had had easier access to all segments of the industry, particularly those with higher status, but our difficulties with volunteer recruitment undoubtedly narrowed our vision of a diverse phenomenon. If street hustlers and Outcasts are so well represented among our respondents, for example, it is partly because the twenty dollars' compensation we offered for an interview was about equal to the amount they stood to lose by giving us an hour of their time, while it paled in comparison to the substantial earning power of strippers and escorts. Other categories of sex workers we were unable to interview included certain types of male models, young artists looking to be "discovered," and high-level bodybuilders; ads in magazines targeting male or gay audiences suggest that these three categories of rent boys are also available and in demand.

But we shall leave to others the further exploration of the territory we have charted with the time and resources at our disposal. It will be a challenge, for this world of the clandestine and the unspoken does not yield up its secrets easily. Much remains to be discovered with regard not only to the workers themselves but also to the sex entrepreneurs and clients who live from and for the male sex trade. Now as ever, what is dubiously called "the world's oldest profession" is still a mystery to many, especially when its practitioners are men.

Notes

1 Michel Dorais with Denis Ménard, *Les enfants de la prostitution.*

2 This study was conducted with the help of a team of master's and doctoral students at Université Laval consisting, at various times, of Ginette Paré, Olivier Charron, and Patrick Berthiaume, principally for the interviews, with Simon Louis Lajeunesse involved at the data analysis stage.

3 See Michel Dorais, *Don't Tell: The Sexual Abuse of Boys.*

4 Although it does exist in North America, transvestite prostitution appears to represent a much smaller proportion of the male sex trade than in France, for example, where it occupies a sizable share of the market; see Daniel Welzer-Lang with Odette Barbosa and Lilian Mathieu, *Prostitution: Les uns, les unes et les autres.*

5 A good summary of these matters can be found in the special issue of *L'Histoire* no. 264, April 2002,

titled "Le commerce du sexe"; see also the chapter titled "Une bien vieille histoire" in *Les enfants de la prostitution* for further relevant information on the history of prostitution.

6 In *Entre père et fils: La prostitution homosexuelle des garçons.*

7 In *Sexual Variance in Society and History.*

8 See chapter 5 of Michel Dorais, *Éloge de la diversité sexuelle.*

9 Robin Lloyd, *For Money or Love: Boy Prostitution in America.*

10 *Gay New York*, 67.

11 *For Money or Love.*

12 Mack Friedman, *Strapped for Cash: A History of American Hustler Culture.*

13 See, for example, C.A. Tripp, *The Homosexual Matrix.*

14 *Outsiders: Studies in the Sociology of Deviance.*

15 See *Sexual Meanings and Safer Sex Practices.*

16 In *Séropositifs: Trajectoires identitaires et rencontres du risque*, 27.

17 Unlike contemporary western cultures, certain ancient or oriental cultures had boarding schools where girls and boys, usually slaves or children of modest families, learned the prostitute's trade.

18 Peep-shows allow adult clients sitting in private booths to watch porno films or, in some cases, live strip acts behind a window. Short segments are shown to entice the client, who must continually drop money in the machine if he wants the show to go on.

19 Tubiana, *L'Éducation et la vie*, 152.

20 See "La sexualité à risque existe-t-elle?," in *Un sujet inclassable? Approches sociologiques, littéraires et juridiques des homosexualités*, 157.

21 "Une autre forme de rationalité: Les mécanismes de protection imaginaire et symbolique," 65–76.

22 David Le Breton, *Passions du risque*.

23 See also on this subject Richard R. Pleak and Heino F. L. Meyer-Bahlburg, "Sexual Behavior and AIDS Knowledge of Young Male Prostitutes in Manhattan": 557–87, and C.A. Rietmeijer, "Sex Hustling, Injection Drug Use, and Non-Gay Identification by Men Who Have Sex with Men: Associations with High-Risk Sexual Behaviors and Condom Use": 353–60.

24 On this subject, see M.B. Sycamore, *Tricks and Treats*, a collection of writings by sex workers about their clients; see also the innovative research done in Australia by Victor Minichiello et al., particularly "A Profile of the Clients of Male Sex Workers in Three Australian Cities": 511–18, which derived its data from detailed diaries kept by sex workers.

25 A few "roles" may be reserved for older boys: sexually initiating younger boys, for instance, or participating in certain ring activities (for example, a client wanting several boys for group sex). The purpose of this is to keep a degree of control over the boys and ensure their silence.

Bibliography

Adam, Barry et al. *Sexual Meanings and Safer Sex Practices*. Report submitted to Health Canada, 1998.

Becker, Howard. *Outsiders: Studies in the Sociology of Deviance*. New York: Free Press 1966.

Bochow, Michael. "La sexualité à risque existe-t-elle?" In *Un sujet inclassable? Approches sociologiques, littéraires et juridiques des homosexualités*, edited by Rommel Mendès-Leite. Lille: Gai Kitsch Camp 1995.

Bullough, Vern L. *Sexual Variance in Society and History*. Chicago: University of Chicago Press 1976.

Chauncey, George. *Gay New York*. New York: Basic Books 1994.

Delor, François. *Séropositifs: Trajectoires identitaires et rencontres du risque*. Paris: L'Harmattan 1997.

Dorais, Michel. *Don't Tell: The Sexual Abuse of Boys*. Translated by Isabel Denholm Meyer. Montreal and Kingston: McGill-Queen's University Press 2002.

– *Éloge de la diversité sexuelle*. Montreal: VLB Éditeur 1999.

Dorais, Michel, and Denis Ménard. *Les enfants de la prostitution*. Montreal: VLB Éditeur 1987.

Friedman, Mack. *Strapped for Cash: A History of American Hustler Culture*. Los Angeles: Alyson 2003.

Gauthier-Hamon, Corinne, and Roger Teboul. *Entre père et fils: La prostitution homosexuelle des garçons*. Paris: PUF 1988.

Le Breton, David. *Passions du risque*. Paris: Métailié 2000.

Lloyd, Robin. *For Money or Love: Boy Prostitution in America*. New York: Vanguard Press 1976.

Mendès-Leite, Rommel. "Une autre forme de rationalité: Les mécanismes de protection imaginaire et symbolique." In *Les homosexuels face au sida: Rationalités et gestions des risques,* edited by Marcel Calvez, Marie-Ange Schlitz, and Yves Souteyrand. Paris: Agence Nationale de Recherches sur le Sida, 1996.

Minichiello, Victor, et al. "A Profile of the Clients of Male Sex Workers in Three Australian Cities." *Public Health* 23, no. 5 (1999).

Pleak, Richard R., and Heino F.L. Meyer-Bahlburg. "Sexual Behavior and AIDS Knowledge of Young Male Prostitutes in Manhattan." *Journal of Sex Research* 27, no. 4 (1990): 557–87.

Rietmeijer, C.A. "Sex Hustling, Injection Drug Use, and Non-Gay Identification by Men Who Have Sex with Men: Associations with High-Risk Sexual Behaviors and Condom Use." *Sexually Transmitted Diseases* 25, no. 7 (1998): 353–60.

Sycamore, M.B. *Tricks and Treats*. Binghamton: Harrington Park Press 2000.

Tripp, C.A. *The Homosexual Matrix*. New York: Meridian 1987.

Tubiana, Maurice. *L'Éducation et la vie*. Paris: Odile Jacob 1999.

Welzer-Lang, Daniel, Odette Barbosa, and Lilian Mathieu. *Prostitution: Les uns, les unes et les autres*. Paris: Métailié 1994.

Index